THE POWER OF
HIS RESURRECTION

by

E. K. ELLIS
*Vicar of Boston and
Canon of Lincoln*

THE FAITH PRESS
7 TUFTON STREET LONDON S.W. I

FIRST PUBLISHED IN 1962

© E. K. Ellis, 1962

PRINTED IN GREAT BRITAIN
in 10 point Baskerville type
BY THE FAITH PRESS LTD
LEIGHTON BUZZARD

STUDIES IN CHRISTIAN FAITH
AND PRACTICE

4

THE POWER OF HIS RESURRECTION

PREFACE

MANY people think that the Christian Religion is founded, for the most part, on mere supposition; but they are very much mistaken. The Christian Religion is founded on knowledge. It is true that it is also founded on faith. It has to be, for it is concerned with many matters which cannot be tested by the outward senses. But that does not mean that Christian believers are people who base their lives on pious fancies or on guess-work. The basis of the Christian life is 'the *knowledge* and love of God, and of his Son, Jesus Christ.'

A whole-hearted belief in Jesus as incarnate God and the Saviour of men brings an experience which is as real as anything else in life. Wherever that belief has been accepted it has left a mark on human life and character which cannot be mistaken. Christians claim that this belief has been by far the greatest influence for good in the history of the world.

It seems clear to us that the world of our time has gone wrong by attempting to ignore these facts—well-established facts of experience and of history. The world has advanced to new knowledge, but in doing so it has turned away from an older knowledge which is equally authentic and certainly not less important.

By sharing in the community-experience which results from belief in Christ, we learn to recognize the Christian Revelation as a system of teaching which comes from a higher source than Man. We find in it something which stands in strong contrast to the gropings of the human mind—something which is quite distinct from those human ideas of truth which change from age to age, and indeed from one half-century to another.

The Church was brought into existence by the Resurrection of Jesus, and it is the power of his Resurrection which keeps the Church in existence through the centuries. All that is uniquely Christian, all that Christianity has meant to the human race, all that it has meant in our own lives, reaches us from the risen Christ. It is the power of his Resurrection which has spread the tiny Church of the first Whitsunday over the whole earth, bringing with it a spiritual insight, a beauty of life and character, and a hope for the future such as the world had never known before and can find nowhere else.

When St. Paul wrote that he counted everything else as worthless 'that I may know him and the power of his Resurrection,' he was already living by that power; yet his one hope in life was to advance in a knowledge which he felt to be boundless (Phil. 3). All this remains as it was, whatever the response of our own generation may be. Christ's Manhood, risen, glorified and given to men through the Holy Spirit, is the substance of Christian experience and of the Christian life. The accounts of the appearances of the risen Christ which we read in the New Testament were written down, not to convince unbelievers, but to instruct those who already believed. They are intended for the information of people, whether of the first or of the twentieth century, who know something of the power of his Resurrection through their own sharing in the Christian life. They cannot be rightly understood, then, unless they are considered within that setting.

This book aims at nothing more ambitious than to be a simple introduction to the study of Christ's Resurrection. But I have tried to look at the whole of the evidence, including that essential part of it which is to be found in the life of the Church and the experience of the individual believer.

The quotations from the New Testament are taken from the New English Bible, except in a few places (indicated by the letters J.B.P.) in which Mr. J. B. Phillips' translation [1] seemed likely to bring home the meaning more vividly to the general reader, for whom this book is intended.

---

[1] Published by Geoffrey Bles.

CONTENTS

1

DECLARED TO BE THE SON OF GOD
BY A MIGHTY ACT

WAS it possible for a Man who was incarnate God to rise from the dead? I begin with this question because I am sure that one of the greatest hindrances to Christian belief in our time is a deeply-rooted idea that the Resurrection of Jesus is incredible.

Of course there are those who do not believe it because they do not wish it to be true. That attitude has always been possible, and from the first there have been some who have chosen it. But this book is written for those who do wish to believe and who perhaps for that very reason are inclined to exaggerate the difficulties rather than to underestimate them. For their purpose the first necessity is to drag out into the light, and to face squarely, this idea of *impossibility* which haunts the darker corners of the twentieth-century mind.

It may be a help, in the first place, to point out that there is really nothing specifically modern in this idea. It is not based on any new knowledge, which was hidden from our Christian forefathers, but on the unreasoned assumption that the evidence for an exceptional event must be suspected to be unreliable, and that a unique event is incredible. 'When Paul spoke of a resurrection of the dead, some mocked.' That was the reaction more than nineteen hundred years ago, at the very beginning of the growth of Christian belief.

It is a natural first reaction, for people of all times. Incredulity was the first reaction of the disciples themselves. It appears to have been quite as difficult to convince them of the fact of their Master's Resurrection as it would have been to convince any average man of the twentieth century in their place. They were certainly not expecting it.

We know what their state of mind was on the Friday evening, and all through the hours of the following day. 'He that is hanged on a tree is accursed of God,' said the Old Testament. 'Take the body down before the Sabbath begins, lest the sight of that accursed thing should profane God's holy day.' (Deut. 21 : 23; Mark 15 : 42, 43; John 19 : 40–2.) So the little group of broken-hearted and broken-spirited men and women had taken the Body down hurriedly, wrapped it in linen cloths with aromatic gums strewn in the folds, and placed it in a sepulchre which had been offered for the purpose and which was close at hand. There they had to leave it because it was Friday evening and the beginning of the Sabbath. And then there was complete despair, hopeless sorrow, fear of God and fear of men, in that upper room with the locked doors.

His enemies had said 'Let him come down from the cross, and we will believe him! For he said, I am the Son of God.' There seemed to be no answer to that. God had refused to accept him. God had not delivered him. His Body lay in the sepulchre, drained of blood, the arms pulled out of joint, hands and feet gashed with the wounds of the nails, a circle of red scars round the brow, the back scored with the weals of the scourging, and a gaping spear-wound in the side. It seemed as final as anything in this world can be. The authorities considered this little group of men so unimportant that it was not worth the trouble to search them out and arrest them. If nothing else had happened, we can be sure they would before long have separated and gone back to their homes and their fishing boats. There would have been no Christian Church, and therefore there could have been no Christian Religion.

But something did happen. A short time later, we find these same men changed, in a way which needs to be accounted for ; possessed by a message which they felt bound to share with others, first with their fellow-Jews, later with men of all nations and of all kinds; willing to be mocked and beaten and tortured for that message; willing to die for it. And for some reason (which also needs to be accounted for) these plain, uncultured men were able to bear their witness so convincingly that, wherever they went, there were some who believed.

Those who believed were changed too. Wealthy men sold their goods and gave the proceeds to the poor. Men and women dedicated their lives to the service of others. Those who had been cruel became tender-hearted and merciful. Those who had been sensual became chaste, unselfish, spiritually minded. The world began to see a pattern of human life which was quite new—men and women praying for their murderers, returning good for evil and blessing for cursing, making it their business to care for the diseased and the destitute with whom they had no natural concern, even collecting the unwanted babies who had been left by the road-side to die.

Everything was against the spreading of this message and of the new life which accompanied it—the almost unlimited power of the Roman State (for nearly three hundred years, to profess Christianity was a crime for which death was the legal penalty), the sneers of the learned men who moulded the opinions of the world in those centuries, the hatred of the pleasure-loving crowds who could so easily be led to set up a cry of 'The Christians to the lions!', in fact, the whole combined strength and cunning of unredeemed human nature.

Every man who became a Christian knew that he was accepting the danger of persecution. From that day onward, he would never be free from the risk of sudden arrest, trial, and the severe penalties of the law, which included the most brutal forms of torture. Yet the Faith continued to spread, from man to man, from city to city. It crossed the seas and mountain barriers. St. Irenaeus, who lived and wrote in the second century, could speak of 'the Church now spread throughout the whole world.' He could point out that 'although the languages differ, yet the teaching of the tradition is one and the same. The churches which have been planted in Germany do not believe anything different, nor do those in Spain, in Gaul, in the East, in Egypt, in Lybia.' (*Adv. Haer.* I, 10.) Though their numbers were continually being reduced by martyrdom, the Christians continued to multiply. At the end of three hundred years, the greatest totalitarian state of the ancient world had been compelled, by the sheer weight of their numbers, to submit to them.

What was it, then, which changed the lives of these men and women who became Christians, giving them a spirit and an outlook which were quite new in this world, driving them on to attempt apparent impossibilities and to accomplish them? There is no doubt about the answer. All the evidence makes it clear that it was an overmastering certainty that the Leader in whom they believed had risen from the dead.

To suppose that, while all this was happening, the Body of Jesus was in fact decaying in the tomb, or that his first disciples had not seen and spoken to him after his death, and been given proofs that his claims were vindicated, would be to suppose something that is more difficult to believe than it is to believe that the Resurrection took place. The rapid spreading of the Faith, in the first three centuries, is a fact which needs to be accounted for.

It is not 'impossible' that God should become Man, or that the human race should have been provided with a Saviour. True, his Resurrection was a unique happening. It was neither the appearance of a spirit nor the mere reanimation of a dead body. It has never been claimed, or imagined, that anything exactly similar has happened to any one else, either before or since. But Jesus was, by nature, a unique Person. No one else has been like him in the life that he lived and the claims that he made.

What, then, is the real message of this unique event? What does it tell us about him? He is 'declared to be the Son of

God by a mighty act, in that he rose from the dead.' (Rom. 1 : 4.) He has been proved to be what he claimed to be.

The Easter message is not simply a message of survival. Evil men, as well as the good, survive the death of the body. This natural fact has nothing to do with the Resurrection of our Lord, and very little to do with the purpose of his post-resurrection appearances.

He came back, not to show that there is a life after death, but to show that he himself is the Son of God, as he claimed to be. He was put to death for making that claim. He was 'declared to *be* the Son of God by a mighty act, in that he rose from the dead.'

It was a great victory. We have seen other victories in our time, and have shared in the rejoicing. But somehow they have not made things so much better as we hoped they would. The victory that we commemorate at Easter was decisive. Nothing can reverse it.

It brings the one message that is most needed at this present time—an assurance which we can grasp, and hold fast. We live in an age that is overshadowed by fear. 'Men faint with terror at the thought of all that is coming upon the world.' (Luke 21 : 26.) There may be good reason for those fears. But at least we need have no fears for our Religion. He who rose from the dead is able to preserve his Church, the Body through which he now expresses himself in this world. Those who ever feel inclined to shake their heads and say 'I'm afraid the Cause is lost!' should remember how hopelessly lost that Cause seemed to be on the first Good Friday evening. Since the first Easter Day every believer, through the power of Christ alone, shares in his Master's victory.

Death, destruction, brutality, denial of all higher values—these hideous powers which seem to have been unleashed in the world of our time are swallowed up in the Easter victory. On the other hand all those things that Christians have learnt to love best, to esteem and to reverence—justice, truth, mercy, unselfishness, beauty in thought, in art, in character, ideals

13

of human life which rise far above the levels of the merely animal part of our nature—it is because Jesus rose from the dead that we know these things are secure. If they are driven out of any part of the world for a time, they will come back. We believe these things have always been secure in that world which lies beyond the reach of our five senses. But it was for this familiar world, this world in which we are living now, that the victory needed to be won and has been won.

2

THE IRREVERSIBLE VICTORY

'I passed on to you Corinthians first of all the message I had myself received—that Christ died for our sins, as the Scriptures said he would; that he was buried, and rose again on the third day, again as the Scriptures foretold. He was seen by Cephas, then by the Twelve, and later he was seen simultaneously by over five hundred Christians, of whom the majority are still alive, though some have since died. He was then seen by James, then by all the Apostles, and last of all, as if to one born abnormally late, he appeared to me.' (1 Cor. 15 : 3 to 8.[1])

These words are specially interesting and important because they are, beyond any doubt, an expression of the primitive Christian belief. They embody the message that was given, in a more or less fixed form of words, to all who wished to become Christians, at the time when the Christian Religion was just beginning. If you like to put it in that way, this was the first Christian Creed.

The facts are well established. The First Epistle to the Corinthians was written about the year 57—that is, about as near to the date of the Crucifixion of Christ as we are to the beginning of the Second World War. They were written by a man who had become a convert to Christianity a few years after the Crucifixion. Since then, he had travelled in several countries, making many hundreds of converts. He had spent some time at Corinth, where there was now a flourishing Christian community. He had been away from them for some years; and now the news that reached him made it necessary

[1] This is J. B. Phillips' translation, which seems in this place to be clearer than the version in the New English Bible.

for him to write to the Church at Corinth about certain matters which needed to be set in order. He says, then, 'When I was with you I *began* by passing on to you the message that was given to me, when I first became a Christian.' We remind ourselves that St. Paul's conversion happened only a few years after the Crucifixion of our Lord. And we have seen what this message was, this accepted form of Christian belief which was passed on to all Christian converts.

It is obviously untrue, then, to say that belief in the Resurrection of Jesus grew up gradually, as a demi-god myth or a mere legend might have grown. *That* explanation, at least, is impossible. It would have been easy to believe that Jesus was merely a good man, who remained dead in the way that other good men remain dead, but that in course of time superstitious tales grew up and passed round among his followers, until at last they began to say that he had risen from the dead. That would be easy : but the evidence and the dates rule out that explanation. However the Christian Faith came into existence ; we can be quite certain that things did not happen in that way.

On the contrary, it was an overwhelming conviction that Jesus had risen from the dead which *started* the Christian Religion. This little group of believers—the 'Apostles,' as we call them—*began* their task by telling people that they knew, without any possibility of mistake, that their Master had risen on the third day after his death. The consequence had been that they had found all their ideas turned upside down, and had realized that a message was entrusted to them which they were bound to pass on to others and to spread through the whole world.

Let us look at this message again. It was not the substance of 'the sermon on the mount.' It made no mention of the moral teachings of Jesus, or of his works of healing. It did not even begin with belief in God. It was this—'Christ died for our sins, and he was buried' (this was mentioned to make it clear that he really died—he had been 'dead and buried,'

16

as we say); 'and rose again on the third day' (that is, his Resurrection was not merely the appearance of a departed spirit to loved ones left behind in this world). The rest of the message, as we have seen, was simply a list of those who saw him after his Resurrection and it included a mention of over five hundred who had all seen him on one and the same occasion—'the majority of whom,' wrote St. Paul about twenty-five years later, 'are still living, though some have since died.'

It is for those who deny the Resurrection of Jesus to produce some other rational explanation of how these words came to be written, and accepted, at this date.

To us this evidence means just what it meant to the first believers. The power of Evil, and incidentally the power of Evil as it manifests itself in human death, is broken. When we bury our loved ones, we do not suppose that we have parted with them for ever. Since Jesus has conquered death, 'God will just as surely bring with Jesus all who are "asleep" in him.' (1 Thess. 4: 14; J.B.P.) Exactly how this will happen, we neither know nor expect to know. That it will happen seems to us a natural inference, as it did to the first Christians.

But the essence of the message for us, as it was for them, is that our Lord's Resurrection has set up a new Kingdom of God on earth, of which we are members. We are compelled to see in the Resurrection of Christ an act of God himself, bringing about a new 'break' in the history of this world; opening a new way of progress to the human race; a conquest of evil which is in some degree repeated in the lives of countless men and women, through their relationship with the risen Christ.

The Resurrection of Jesus was a decisive victory over Evil. One who lived only for his Father's will, who never pleased himself, who 'went about doing good,' had been put to an agonizing and shameful death. Even to his followers, that seemed to be the end. When the cold, stiffening Body was released from the cross and laid in a tomb, it looked as though God himself had been conquered. But in all this, God

17

was conquering. 'He died for our sins,' said the disciples after his Resurrection. And it is very worthy of note that they said 'He died for *our* sins.' They did not say 'He died for the sins of these wicked people who refuse to believe in him—these people who arrest us and scourge us and put us in prison and try to prevent us from meeting together for our worship.' They said 'He died for *our* sins.'

When he died he was conquering, far more surely than if he had struck his executioners dead and come down from the cross, as they challenged him to do. 'Let the Messiah, the king of Israel, come down now from the cross. If we see that, we shall believe.' (Mark 15 : 32.) How dreadfully those words must have echoed in the minds of his terrified followers! For what answer was there? God was allowing it to happen.

The answer came on the third day. He had not been over-come by Evil. He *actually had* overcome evil with good. They had never thought of that at the time. That was the divine surprise that the first Easter Day brought to those simple, representative men.

He had conquered Evil by submitting freely to the worst that it can do to a man outwardly, without for a moment yielding to it inwardly. The records of his Resurrection day give us a picture of the first Christian witnesses hardly know-ing what to make of an event so unexpected, so astounding; hardly able to accept this truth which was breaking on their minds, that their Master, after all, was alive, triumphant over the powers of Evil, turning the worst that those powers can do into a new assurance of divine forgiveness and of eternal life with God.

'And last of all he appeared to me,' says the writer of the letter which is quoted at the beginning of this chapter. He could say 'I know him,' though he had not known him in the days when Jesus walked among men. By this time many of these Christian converts at Corinth could say the same. 'The second Adam'—the Man who has given the human race this fresh start—'has become a lifegiving Spirit.' It is in that way that we must know him, not as he was in the Gospel days. What Jesus was before his Death and Resurrection must always be a subject of great interest to every Christian, but still only of secondary interest. We are concerned with him not as he was then, but as he is now.

His victory over Evil is repeated, in some measure, in the life of every sincere believer. It has not lost its power through lapse of time. Whatever his personal failures may be, every Christian knows at least that his life has been very different from what it would have been without belief in Christ, without prayer and the sacraments. Except when we fail him and ourselves by turning back from Christ to self, he who conquered Evil in his own Person conquers sin in the Christian. 'He breaks the power of cancelled sin,' as the hymn reminds us.

When we allow the risen Christ to do what we know he wants to do with us, when a new spirit begins to rule in our minds, cleaning out the dark corners, causing our trust and our pride to centre in him instead of in ourselves, showing us plainly that God-service and not self-service ought to be the ruling motive of our lives—then we know the Lord of Easter in the way in which he wills us to know him. Then the Resurrection of Jesus touches us too, as it has so many before us, and we in our turn are lifted and carried by the tide of that Life.

3

'GO TO MY BROTHERS'

THERE are few accounts, even of perfectly natural happenings, that bear the stamp of truth more plainly than the account in St. John's Gospel of certain events which took place on the first Easter morning. (John 20 : 1–18.)

Let us imagine ourselves standing outside the tomb of Jesus early in the morning of that day, and see what happens.

For a while the garden is deserted. There is silence, except for the twittering of the birds. A group of women who came at daybreak to embalm the Body have gone back to tell the disciples that they found the heavy circular stone rolled away from the entrance to the sepulchre, and the sepulchre empty. They said further that they had seen a vision of angels, but the disciples did not pay much attention to that. They were troubled by the report that the Body was no longer in the tomb. But the 'vision of angels, who said that he was alive' might be a mere effect of the imagination of these women, who were obviously excited and afraid. So 'their words seemed to them like idle tales.' These details are from other Gospels. Now we can turn to St. John.

One of the women, Mary Magdalene, had gone specially to tell Peter and John ; so Peter and John set out to see for themselves what had happened. Let us get back, then, to our place in the garden.

Presently there is a sound of footsteps, of men running. It is not yet broad daylight, so it is not until they are close to the tomb that we see the two men. One, who is younger than the other, arrives first, and stands at the entrance of the cave, peering in. Then the other arrives and without any hesitation goes into the sepulchre. The younger man follows him.

They stand there silently for a while in the dim light, lost in their own thoughts. The tomb is empty, as the women had said. But that is not what keeps them standing there, spell-bound with wonder. If that had been all, they would have hurried away again to make enquiries, and to try to discover what had been done with the Master's Body.

They are looking at the grave-cloths, which remain on the ledge of rock where the Body was placed. Who would have stolen the Body and left the grave-cloths? For that matter, it would not have been an easy thing to do, for the aromatic gums which had been strewn on the cloths would cause them to adhere to the skin. It was not likely that any one who wanted to remove the Body would spend time loosening and unwinding the cloths. Even if they had done so, surely the cloths would have been left on the floor of the cave, not re-placed in their original position on the ledge.

But not only did the cloths remain on the ledge where the Body had been placed; they were in a position which sug-gested that they had not been unwound at all. There were the larger cloths, still in their folds. Then there was a space where the neck and lower part of the face had been. And then the smaller cloth, that had been bound like a turban round the head, 'not lying with the other wrappings but rolled together' (or folded round) 'in a place by itself.' The account states this graphic detail quite artlessly. The point is not laboured, nor is its implication stressed. But how could the cloths be in that position, unless the Body had *dematerialized,* and left them to sink down, empty but still in their folds, on the shelf of rock?

At length, still in silence, the two men come out of the sepulchre to return home. They say no word to Mary Mag-dalene, who has followed them to the garden and stayed out-side the cave. Unlike her, they are no longer anxious to make enquiries as to what has become of the Body.

Presently, Mary stoops and looks into the cave. The position of the grave-cloths conveys nothing to her. Her one thought is that the Master's Body has been taken away, and is perhaps being dishonoured or is, at least, among strangers, who do not care about him. Her one hope is to discover where the Body has been placed, so that she may give it reverent burial and still be able to visit his tomb. In the excess of her love and grief, she imagines herself to be strong enough, somehow or other, to perform this task unaided. 'If it is you, sir, who removed him, tell me where you have laid him, and I will take him away.' Lest we should think her unobservant and unspiritual, at this moment she is given her own vision of angels.

She sees a faint, shimmering appearance in the dark cave, like the forms of two men in white, growing more and more distinct, at either end of the ledge of rock. She hears someone say 'Why are you weeping?' She answers, 'Because they have taken away my Lord, and I don't know where they have laid him.' And then she becomes conscious that someone is standing behind her.

In the accounts of the appearances of the risen Christ, we get the impression of an experience which was real and convincing, but which could not be completely and clearly expressed in words. It is natural that this should be so, for words are fitted to express only the normal experiences of life. It is so here. 'As she wept, she peered into the tomb, and she saw two angels in white sitting there, one at the head and one at the feet, where the Body had lain.' 'She turned round and saw Jesus standing there, but did not recognize him.' As we read these accounts, we are in a borderland which lies between familiar things and another condition of life, into which Jesus has passed. A reality from beyond the physical world was manifesting itself to the senses in these men and women who were the first witnesses of the Resurrection.

Their accounts impress us, above all, by their *artlessness*. The apparently contradictory details are recorded simply, and without comment. His Body could be touched and felt. He asked for food, and ate it in the presence of the disciples. Yet he had appeared among them suddenly, in a room where the doors were locked, and he disappeared as suddenly. His Heart had been pierced by the blade of a spear, and the wound remained in his side. None the less, he was alive. He knew what the doubting disciple had been saying, although he had not been visibly present when the words were spoken, and he did not reappear at once to remove his doubts. In all this we recognize something essentially different from the kind of detail that pious imagination would have invented.

So when he appeared to Mary Magdalene, at first she did not know him. It was her own name, 'Mary,' spoken in his own voice, which brought recognition, although it meant recognizing that 'the impossible' had become the real. As she flings herself down to clasp his Feet, she is content to call him by the old name of 'Master.' She still thinks of him merely as the human Master, somehow, in ways beyond hope or belief, restored to her alive. How natural it was that she should wish to make sure of him by clinging desperately to his Feet!

She will have to rise to a higher knowledge—to know he is close to her without being able to see him or to hold him; to obey and follow him without hearing his voice. But meanwhile, he gives her something to do. 'Do not cling to me, for I have not yet ascended to the Father. But go to my brothers and tell them, I am now ascending to my Father and your Father, my God and your God.' (John 20 : 17.)

In accordance with the ideas of that time, the disciples would not accept a woman as a witness. Mary could not be included among the commissioned witnesses who would proclaim Christ's Resurrection to the world. The message given to her was for the disciples themselves. And although they would not admit that her testimony deserved to be believed, yet it must have prepared their minds, to some extent, for the shock of the risen Master's first appearance to them.

On every Sunday in the year, the Church throughout all the world is filled with the fragrance of the Easter message. 'Jesus is a living Person, divine and human. Through the faith

23

and worship of the Church, through prayer and the sacraments, we can make contact with him ; and this contact with a Leader who has conquered death can transform the lives of men and women.'

If this is real to us, we must pass on the message to others. It was in that way that Christianity began, and in that way that we ourselves received it. However unworthy of the task we may feel, we are bound to be ready to tell other people about the Saviour of the human race, and about the life of his Church, through which he himself is still active in this world. Because we possess free will, his action must depend on man's co-operation. Because we possess free will there have been, and perhaps always will be, false and insincere Christians among the members of his Church. But every one who will respond in faith and loyalty becomes an agent through whom the risen Christ carries on his work; and on that work the welfare of the human race depends, in this world as well as in the life beyond death.

In England at the present time, there is a great need for witness—firm, unpretentious, as matter-of-fact as we can make it. So many people have been conditioned to think that they can find complete satisfaction in the things of this world alone —their work, their recreation, their money, their daily newspaper, their television set, their family and social relationships. They seem to feel no need for contact with anything higher than the things of this world. Yet they are capable of fellowship with God ; designed for an eternal life with God.

For all these people, and they must be numbered in millions, life could be more worth while, happier, filled with a purpose and meaning which would completely transform it. They need the risen Christ. And he needs them. He is longing that the latent gifts of baptism, which most of them have received, should be awakened in them, so that he may use them in his service. Perhaps he could use some of them more effectually than he can use us who are already practising Churchpeople.

'Go to my brothers.' There is a confused idea in their minds that Christian belief is outmoded, that it is not for these times, that something which they vaguely call 'Science' has displaced it, if not disproved it. Let them know, then, that you find values in your religion which no scientific theories or mechanical inventions can supply. At least offer them your fellowship, if they seem willing to enquire into these things for themselves.

Perhaps our fellowship is what will help them most. We need not pretend to know the answers to all their questions, nor expect them to agree with all our opinions. But if they seem prepared to listen, we can find something to tell them, surely, about beliefs which mean so much to us that we cannot even imagine what life would be like without them.

4

THE RISEN CHRIST IN THE
EUCHARIST

BELIEF in the Resurrection of Jesus is not usually built on the accounts of his post-Resurrection appearances alone. In fact I suppose it is doubtful whether any unbeliever, after reading these accounts in the Gospels, has ever felt bound to say 'This evidence proves conclusively that Jesus rose from the dead; therefore I must become a Christian.'

Some may have been brought to belief by reading the New Testament as a whole. That is a different matter. But usually the community of believers has played some part in the conversion, even if it has been represented only by one person, or by the records of Christian lives that have been lived in the past. What normally happens is that belief in the Resurrection of Jesus grows out of the believer's personal contacts with the Church. It is natural that it should happen in this way, for the Church owes its existence to the Lord's Resurrection. It began its world-wide growth by proclaiming his Resurrection. It is by the power of his Resurrection that the Church lives on through the centuries.

The Gospel accounts of the post-Resurrection appearances were written for men and women who already believed that Jesus had risen from the dead. These men and women would have said without hesitation that they knew him as a living Saviour. But each of the accounts had something to teach them, and has something to teach us, about the Christian's relationships with that Saviour.

The Eucharist is one means by which each member of the Church shares in the Church's contact with the risen Christ. In the first place, the mere existence of this form of worship, in all ages and in all lands which the religion of the cross has reached, is an evidence of the Resurrection because, from the first and always, it has taken the form of thanksgiving, as the very name 'Eucharist' denotes. It could not have had this meaning for the disciples if their Master's Crucifixion had been the last they saw of him. In that case it would have been, at best, what is known to-day as a 'Memorial Service,' or respectful commemoration of the departed. Indeed, it would have been something even more depressing than that, for it could only have brought back memories of their Master's failure and their own.

In the Eucharist one cannot escape from the memory of the death of Christ. The Body and the Blood are separated, as they were separated in death. Yet from the first this Breaking of the Bread was spoken of as the Thanksgiving ('Eucharistia' in the Greek). It was a memorial not of a dead Master, but of a Master who had died and yet had triumphed over death.

The way in which this distinctively Christian worship was regarded from the beginning, then, is in itself an impressive, undesigned evidence of the Resurrection. Writing not more than twenty-five years after the first Good Friday, St. Paul says 'When we break the bread, is it not a means of sharing in the Body of Christ?' (1 Cor. 10 : 16.) It is clear that when he wrote those words St. Paul was not propounding a novel theory or imparting new information. He was referring to a belief so universally accepted by Christians that he could make it the subject of a rhetorical question.

Notice too that this was a belief in a communion (or a 'sharing,' as N.E.B. translates it) of the Body of Christ, not merely of the Spirit of Christ. If the Body of Jesus had decayed in the tomb, as the bodies of other prophets and religious teachers had done, then his disciples might still have spoken of holding communion with his Spirit. They might conceivably have believed that they could hold communion with his Spirit by meeting together to receive bread and wine in his memory. But to call this 'a means of sharing in his Body' would have been an unnatural misuse of words.

The account of the appearance of Jesus to two disciples at Emmaus, during the afternoon of the first Easter Day, illustrates several truths which have played an important part in Christian belief. One of these is the truth of the real Presence of the risen Christ in the Eucharist. (Luke 24 : 13–35.)

These two disciples were walking northward from Jerusalem to Emmaus, where they lived. As they walked, they were talking about the crucifixion of their Master and the final shattering (as it seemed) of the hopes which they had placed in him.

Suddenly they were aware of a third person, walking beside them. He asked them what they were discussing, and why they were sad. Their minds were so full of the subject, and the New-comer had seemed to join them in such a natural way, that it did not occur to them to be surprised by his presence or to resent his question.

One of them was named Cleopas and it seems a probable guess that it was from him that St. Luke had this account. We can easily imagine Cleopas telling him, 'I said, Are you the only person staying in Jerusalem not to know what has happened there in these last few days?' and St. Luke afterwards writing, 'One of them, whose name was Cleopas, said.' . . . This seems a natural explanation of the way in which the disciple's name is introduced. And incidentally, the man who asked that question would not be likely to forget the rather petulant way in which he had spoken.

However that may be, the narrative is thoroughly convincing. Absorbed in discussing what seems to them the one important happening of the last few days, the men cannot imagine how any one who has been in Jerusalem for the feast should need to be told what they are talking about. The phrases they use to describe their Master and to describe their own hopes are true to the period. They would have been used at that time, but not later, by men who believed in Jesus.

They have been discussing 'all this about Jesus of Nazareth, a prophet powerful in speech and action before God and the whole people.' And they add 'We had been hoping that he was the man to liberate Israel.'

The Stranger offers them an entirely different interpretation of 'what has happened in these last few days.' First he surprises them with the question, 'Was not the Messiah bound to suffer thus before entering into his glory?' Then he explains to them how the Old Testament had foreshadowed a Saviour who would triumph through suffering and death. It was all there, in the sacrifices of the Law, which he had come into the world to fulfil (Matthew 5 : 17, 18) and in the teachings of the prophets, who had been hated while they lived and venerated after their deaths. (Luke 11 : 47–51.) But it had been hidden from them by the self-righteous liberalism of the scribes and Pharisees and by the narrow nationalism in which their minds had been moulded.

The Master himself, when he was still with them, had sometimes spoken to his disciples in this way; but those sayings of his had seemed at the time obscure or incredible. What they implied had been so contrary to the disciples' way of thinking that it had only frightened them. (Mark 10 : 32.) A crucified Messiah! The warnings he had given about what was going to happen had seemed to them gloomy forebodings of defeat. Peter had even ventured to rebuke him for speaking in that way. (Matthew 16 : 22.)

But if he had risen from the dead, then of course his rejection and his shameful death would wear an entirely different aspect. . . . The women 'who went early to the tomb returned with a story that they had seen a vision of angels, who told them he was alive.' The tomb was empty. 'Some of our people' had gone to the sepulchre and verified that fact. Neither that fact, however, nor the women's story of their vision had led them to accept an explanation which seemed, on the face of it, quite incredible.

But this Stranger was so certain about it! And as they

listened to him, his interpretation of the Scriptures made this explanation seem more and more likely to be true. The Messiah had conquered evil, then, by taking its full weight upon himself—even the curse of the cross, even the humiliation of death and burial—and had risen in the power of a new life which is beyond the reach of all that evil can do. No wonder that 'they felt their hearts on fire'!

Almost before they realized it, they were entering the village; and the Stranger apparently intended to leave them and continue his journey. They urged him to stay, to go with them into the house. 'Evening draws on,' they said, 'and the day is almost over.' Those phrases need not imply much more than it was after noon. They were pleading a case. There was still time for these two disciples to return to Jerusalem with their news before the risen Master appeared, that same evening, in the Upper Room.

It was because they were so eager to keep him with them that the Stranger seemed to change his mind, and came into the house. The most surprising fact in this narrative is that, throughout all this time, they had not recognized him. Here is something that needs explaining, for we are considering an event which really happened.

These two did not belong to the inner circle—'the Eleven.' Apparently, since they lived at Emmaus, they did not even belong to the company of men and women who had followed Jesus from Galilee. But they were accepted as members of the band of believers. They had heard about the empty tomb and the story told by the women. They could speak quite naturally of 'some women of our company' and 'some of our people.' They were admitted at once to the room where the disciples were waiting behind locked doors; and before they could begin their own story they were told that the Lord had appeared to Peter.

They must, then, have known the Master well enough to recognize his appearance and his voice without any difficulty. One would have expected, in fact, that under normal conditions they would recognize him immediately. Yet although he had walked beside them and talked to them for a considerable time (as the account implies that he did) they had not recognized him.

This problem appears independently in almost all the accounts of the risen Christ. It is obviously important. And it seems obvious too that this difficulty about recognition, this doubt as to his identity, even among those who knew and loved him best, would not have been invented or stressed by narrators whose main object was to strengthen belief in the Lord's Resurrection. This puzzling feature, as it appears in the various records, stamps them as coming from truthful witnesses, who mention everything that seems important, just as they saw or heard it.

Why did Mary Magdalene, instead of recognizing the risen Master at once, suppose him to be the Gardener? (John 20 : 15.) Why did he need to tell the disciples in the Upper Room, 'It is I myself'? (Luke 24 : 12.) Why did the disciples want to ask him 'Who are you?' when he came to them on the shore of the Sea of Galilee? (John 21 : 12). How did it happen that 'some were doubtful' (Matt. 28 : 17) when he appeared to a company of disciples on the mountain in Galilee where he had promised to meet them? Why did these two fail to recognize him, not only when he was walking with them to Emmaus but also, at first, when he entered the house with them? It may be said that Mary was blinded by her tears; that the disciples in the Upper Room were terrified by what they took to be a ghostly apparition; that when they saw him on the sea-shore it was by the dim light of dawn; that you would need to look more than once before you could recognize a person whom you knew had been dead and buried, because what we see or fail to see depends to some extent on what we consider to be possible.

But when all this has been said, we are left with the feeling that it does not fully explain this difficulty in recognition. The accounts seem to imply that the Lord's outward appear-

ance had changed, and also perhaps that the sense-percep-
tions of the disciples were affected in some abnormal way
during the times when he was with them. It is the latter explanation that St. Luke gives in this account. He says simply
that 'something held their eyes from seeing who it was' (v. 16).

Recognition came when the Stranger repeated the actions
of the Eucharist. 'When he had sat down with them at table,
he took bread and said the blessing; he broke the bread and
offered it to them.' Although these two had not been present
at the Last Supper, it is natural to suppose that they had been
told about the institution of the Eucharist. And at this moment
it happened that 'their eyes were opened and they recognized
him; and he vanished from their sight.' They were left with
the broken bread before their eyes, and the sense of an unseen Presence which could still be with them, though the
Master's visible Presence had been withdrawn.

This was news that must be told. So 'without a moment's
delay they set out and returned to Jerusalem. There they
found that the Eleven and the rest of the company had
assembled, and were saying "It is true : the Lord has risen;
he has appeared to Simon." Then they gave their account of
the events of their journey and told how he had been recognized by them at the breaking of the bread.'

This real though unseen Presence of the risen Lord still
remains with us in the Eucharist. St. Irenaeus, writing in the
second century expresses the primitive belief in these words,
'Whenever the cup that man mixes and the bread that man
makes receive the invocation of God, the Eucharist becomes
the Body of Christ.' (*Adv. Haer.* V. 2, 3.) For that matter, it
had been clearly expressed by St. Paul. 'Any one who eats
the bread or drinks the cup unworthily will be guilty of
desecrating the body and blood of the Lord. . . . He who eats
and drinks eats and drinks judgement on himself if he does
not discern the Body.' (1 Cor. 11 : 27, 29.)

A person's body is the sign of his presence. If someone
promises to be 'with us in spirit,' that means that he will not

be actually present, though we might in some way hold communion with him by our thoughts. But the Presence of the risen Christ in the Eucharist does not depend on our thoughts. It depends on his will and his word. If this were not so, the expressions which St. Paul uses in the passage just quoted would be gravely misleading.

If the Presence depended on the communicant's response, a bad communion would be nothing more serious than a missed opportunity or, at most, a misuse of blessed bread and wine. It would not be a desecration of the Body and Blood of the Lord. Nor could we believe that a man brings judgment on himself by failing to discern something that is not real and objective. In that case, in fact, 'discern' would be the wrong word to use. But it is the word which the New Testament uses, and it expresses what has been the Church's belief from the beginning.

As God, the second Person of the Holy Trinity, our Lord is present always and everywhere. But when he met his disciples on the sea-shore (after one of them, at least had addressed him as 'my Lord and my God'), or when he appeared to St. Paul and told him that he was to bear witness in Rome (Acts 23 : 11), here was a special Presence of the Lord, which for the purposes of these men's lives added something new, and very precious, to that truth of the omnipresence of God which they never doubted.

Our Saviour is Man as truly as he is God. He did not become Man only for thirty-three years. In Heaven he still has the Manhood which he derived from his mother. And as Man he is still present with us in this world, 'always, to the end of time.' (Matthew 28 : 20.)

The Presence of God, at all times and in all places, means a great deal to every believing Christian. A habitual remembrance of this great Reality is generally acknowledged to be the most direct means by which any believer can make progress in the devotional life, for a realized fellowship with God is the end and aim of all true devotion.

C

But the Incarnation took place to meet certain specific needs. And because of those needs, the Presence of our Lord's Humanity has a special value for us. Because we are men, we want to kneel to our Good Shepherd, our crucified Saviour, our risen Leader. It is to God-made-Man that we say 'Thou art the King of glory, O Christ; thou art the everlasting Son of the Father. When thou tookest upon thee to deliver man, thou didst not abhor the Virgin's womb. When thou hadst overcome the sharpness of death, thou didst open the kingdom of heaven to all believers. . . . We believe that thou shalt come to be our Judge.'

In the Eucharist our Lord's Manhood, which is in Heaven, is made present to us here in earth. We must of course guard against the idea that Heaven is distant from us, as spatial distances are measured. The Eucharist opens a window for us into the world where Christ's Manhood lives now. When we worship him, present on the altar or in the tabernacle, we are worshipping him present in Heaven. We realize that those phrases 'on the altar' and 'in the tabernacle,' strictly speaking, refer only to the outward sign. The Presence itself is not localized; but he has given us these localized means of admission to his Presence.

> *His manhood pleads where now it lives*
> *On Heaven's eternal throne*
> And *where, in mystic rite, he gives*
> *Its Presence to his own.*

They are not two different Presences, but one and the same. The ancient liturgies speak sometimes of the Body and Blood of Christ as present on the altar, and sometimes of the offerings of bread and wine as taken up to Heaven and there united with his Body and Blood. The Presence of the risen Lord brings the two worlds together, and the consecrated bread of the Eucharist is the point of contact.

'He took bread and said the blessing; he broke the bread, and offered it to them. Then their eyes were opened, and they recognized him; and he vanished from their sight.'

5

THE RISEN CHRIST AS THE
OBJECT OF DIVINE FAITH

A CENTURION of the Roman army, and a group of his relatives and close friends who were living at Caesarea, were the first Gentiles to be converted to Christianity. It was St. Peter who taught them the Faith, and he is reported to have told them about the Resurrection of Jesus in these words. 'God raised him to life on the third day and allowed him to appear, not to the whole people but to witnesses whom God had chosen in advance—to us, who ate and drank with him after he rose from the dead.' (Acts 10 : 40, 41.)

The risen Christ appeared only to those who were qualified to bear faithful witness. It has been through faithful witness that countless thousands of men and women, through the centuries, have come to know the power of his Resurrection. Because the witness was faithful they have learnt to recognize Jesus as the crucified Saviour, the Son of the living God, who gives new life to those who believe in him. Unless they had learnt to think of him in this way it would have been impossible for them to understand the meaning of his Resurrection. In this we can find the reason why he did not appear 'to the whole people, but to witnesses whom God had chosen in advance,' as St. Peter said.

When Jesus appeared to his disciples, late in the evening of the first Easter Day (John 20 : 19), they were already more than half convinced. All through the day the evidence had been building up. First there was the discovery of the empty tomb. There might have been a merely natural explanation for that—though it was not easy to suggest a natural explanation of the position of the grave-clothes. (John 20 : 7.) The women's story of a vision at the tomb 'appeared to be non-sense' (Luke 24 : 11), but the message brought by Mary Magdalene from the risen Lord himself must have made a deeper impression.

It seems to have been St. Peter's account of the Master's appearance to him which had the greatest effect on the minds of the other disciples. As we have seen, when the two dis-ciples from Emmaus returned with the story of their own wonderful experience, they found the others saying 'It is true : the Lord has risen ; he has appeared to Simon.' They had to believe Peter ; and above all they had to believe this changed and humbled Peter who came to them directly from his meeting with the risen Lord, radiant with the knowledge that he was forgiven.

It was while they were still discussing the experience of the disciples from Emmaus that Jesus appeared, 'standing among them.' 'Startled and terrified, they thought they were seeing a ghost,' St. Luke tells us. (24 : 37). That was natural enough, for the doors of the room were locked. (John 20 : 19.)

He told them not to be afraid. 'Why are you so perturbed? Why do questionings arise in your minds? Look at my hands and feet. It is I myself. Touch me and see ; no ghost has flesh and bones, as you can see I have.' (Luke 24 : 38, 39.) He showed them his hands and his side, with the wounds made by the nails and spear. (John 20 : 20.) And at this point in the record there is a simple and vivid comment which, one would say with conviction, comes to us from the memory of one who was actually present at this scene. 'They were still unconvinced, still wondering, *for it seemed too good to be true*.' (Luke 24 : 41.) So he asked them 'Have you anything here to eat?' And when 'they offered him a piece of fish they had cooked, he took it and ate before their eyes.' (vv. 42, 43.)

The properties of the Lord's risen Body must have seemed as inexplicable to these first witnesses as they would seem to the man in the street to-day. In all sincerity they recorded the details which brought to them the certainty that their Master had risen in the power of a new, unearthly life. He appeared to them suddenly, behind locked doors, and disappeared as suddenly ; yet he could eat and drink with them.

It would have been unbelievable except for the evidence of their own senses. But it was characteristic of the Jesus of Bethlehem and Nazareth. And at the moment, nothing could have better served the purpose of making these frightened men feel at ease in his Presence, so far as that was possible. As we have seen, it made such an impression on them that it was this detail which Peter singled out for mention to the first Gentile converts. 'He appeared to witnesses whom God had chosen in advance—to us, who ate and drank with him after he rose from the dead.'

'They offered him a piece of fish they had cooked, which he took and ate before their eyes. And he said to them "This is what I meant by saying, while I was still with you, that everything written about me in the Law of Moses and in the prophets and psalms was bound to be fulfilled." Then he opened their minds to understand the scriptures.'

This part of the Resurrection-message was never overlooked by the first Christian witnesses. There is only one God, and he had revealed himself to Israel in the history and writings of the Old Testament. It was this same God who had 'raised Jesus from the dead'—for that was how they spoke of his Resurrection, just as they spoke of their Master himself as 'the Christ' or 'the Son of God.' Even in those first days they must have realized that he is something more than Man ; but men need time to adjust their minds to new and startling truths. It was not until later that they came to realize, in the full light of Christian experience, that Jesus is God-made-Man—not merely the Son of God, but God the Son ; just as they learnt from Christian experience that the Holy Spirit also is God, the object of divine Faith and worship, equally with the Father and the Son.

This fuller revelation of the Nature and Being of God had

to be received within the framework of the strict monotheism of the Old Testament. When Jesus spoke of 'my Father,' he was speaking of the God who had revealed himself to Israel. 'Both in the Old and New Testament everlasting life is offered to Mankind by Christ, who is the only Mediator between God and Man, being both God and Man.' (Articles of Religion : VII.) Without the Old Testament it would not be possible to understand the New. So all who accepted the Gospel—Romans, Greeks or Egyptians—had to learn something of the history and religion of that small country which, forty years after the Crucifixion of Jesus, was wiped out of existence, but which had been chosen to play a necessary part in the process of God's revelation of himself to men.

Some of the sayings which St. Luke adds to his account of this Easter evening may have been spoken on other occasions. In the first chapter of Acts (v. 3) the same writer says 'he appeared to them over a period of forty days and taught them about the kingdom of God.' But these last verses of his Gospel take us on, without a break, to the command to 'stay here in this city,' the promise of the Holy Spirit, and the Ascension. It seems clear, then, that there is a foreshortening of the historical perspective at this point.

St. John's Gospel records that the evening of Easter Day was the occasion when the risen Christ gave his commission to the Church to speak and act in his Name. The commission was given in a deeply impressive form—first the words 'As my Father sent me, so I send you' : then a symbolical action, 'he breathed on them' ; and finally the words 'Receive the Holy Spirit! If you forgive any man's sins, they stand forgiven ; if you pronounce them unforgiven, unforgiven they remain.' (John 20 : 19–23.)

No doubt it is true that in the last sentence there is a reference to the preaching of the Gospel, followed by the baptism of those who accept it. (Acts 2 : 3 ; 10 : 48 ; 11 : 18.) We still say in the Nicene Creed 'I believe one baptism for the remission of sins.' But there is something more in the words than this. 'If you pronounce them unforgiven, unfor-given they remain.' Those words, taken in their natural sense, imply a commission to give or to withhold absolution in the Name of Christ. The absolution is his alone. 'The Son of man has the right on earth to forgive sins.' (Luke 5 : 24.) But in this matter as in others, he acts through his Church. 'Whatever you forbid on earth shall be forbidden in heaven, and whatever you allow on earth shall be allowed in heaven.' (Matthew 18 : 18.)

In the Anglican Prayer Book these words of commission recorded in St. John's Gospel are the words used in the ordination of priests. 'Receive the Holy Ghost for the office and work of a priest in the Church of God, now committed unto thee by the imposition of our hands. Whose sins thou dost forgive, they are forgiven; and whose sins thou dost retain, they are retained. And be thou a faithful dispenser of the Word of God, and of his holy Sacraments; in the Name of the Father, and of the Son, and of the Holy Ghost. Amen.'

Those words can be regarded as summarizing our beliefs about the Church's Ministry. In the first place, we believe the commission comes from the risen Christ, not in any sense from the men for whom the priest is to minister. The Church is not a man-made institution. It is 'the Church of God,' and there-fore a commission to minister within the Church can be given only by God. It must be the selfsame commission that Christ gave on the first Easter Day. 'As my Father sent me, so I send you.'

In the second place, we believe this commission is passed down from one generation to another through the laying on of hands. The gift of the Holy Spirit for this particular 'office and work in the church of God' does not conflict with those gifts of the Holy Spirit which every member of the Church can receive through faith and prayer, any more than the gift of Easter evening could take the place of the gift of Pente-cost.

Following this passage in St. John's Gospel there is the

account of St. Thomas's profession of faith. (John 20 : 24–9.) In the evening of that first Easter Day, while all this was happening, Thomas had been absent. When he returned, and the others told him 'We have seen the Lord,' he would not believe them. The account does not necessarily imply that he refused to believe they had seen a vision of some kind. But he did refuse to draw the conclusion that the Master had risen from the dead. Nothing that they said could convince him of that.

Thomas seems to have been the type of man who has to make up his mind for himself, and who needs to see every step of the way before he forms a conclusion. (John 14 : 4, 5.) Perhaps it was because he had realized more fully than some of the others what this 'rising from the dead' must mean, that he was so cautious about accepting the fact. However that may be, he withstood all attempts to persuade him, and at last silenced them with the emphatic statement, 'Unless I see the mark of the nails on his hands, unless I put my finger into the place where the nails were, and my hand into his side, I will not believe it.'

A week later, when the disciples were in the room and Thomas with them, although the doors were locked Jesus again stood among them, greeting them with the words 'Peace be with you!' Then he spoke directly to Thomas, 'Reach your finger here : see my hands; reach your hand here and put it into my side; be unbelieving no longer, but believe.' And Thomas answered, 'My Lord, and my God!'

Surely, it was not a sudden change of mind that found expression in those words, but a conviction bred by his own thoughts and his own deep questionings. So far as we know, none of the others had made a profession of faith so full as this, though no doubt this belief was dawning in their minds. It must have been so. They had often heard their Master speak in a way which implied that he was more than Man. They knew that it was for 'blasphemy' that he had been condemned to death in the High Priest's court. (Mark 14 : 63, 64.) It was very clear that his Resurrection had reversed that judgment. They were slow to formulate their full belief in their Lord for an obvious reason. That belief presented great difficulties to the minds of men who had been brought up in the religion of the Old Testament, and who would shrink in horror from the idea of equating any other being with the one God.

But if the truth about the Lord's divine Nature was not plainly stated in the first Christian preaching, it does not follow that this truth was entirely absent from the minds of the preachers. For their purpose it would have been worse than useless to state it, even if they had been sure, at this stage, of the terms in which it should be stated. The men to whom they brought the Gospel had to be led along paths of thought which they could follow. In our Lord's own teaching, the full truth about himself had been implied rather than plainly stated. If he had stated it more plainly he would not have lived to do what had to be done before his Passion.

This profession of faith, then—'My Lord and my God'— was all the more remarkable because it was in advance of its time. Yet Jesus did not greet it with the same eager welcome that he had once given to a profession of faith made by Peter, though Peter had not gone so far as Thomas did. When Jesus had asked his disciples, 'Who do you say that I am?', Peter had answered 'You are the Messiah, the Son of the living God.' And Jesus had said to him, 'Simon, son of Jonah, you are favoured indeed! You did not learn this from mortal man; it was revealed to you by my heavenly Father.' (Matthew 16 : 15–17.)

Peter's confession had been welcomed because it was an example of divine faith—that is, of the understanding and insight which is given by God and must be sought from God. 'It was revealed to you by my heavenly Father.'

We are not required to believe in Jesus without good reasons. There is no merit in being credulous. Nor is that belief to be gained by reasoning alone, or the weighing of evidence alone. It must grow out of our own seeking for a true knowledge of God and God's response to that seeking.

In the days of his ministry our Lord was continually beset by demands for 'a sign,' that is, for some kind of outward proof which would make unbelief impossible. St. Thomas's demand did not sink to that level. It was natural that he should want to see the Lord himself, as the others had done. And being the man he was, it was natural that he should want to be certain that this mysterious person really was the Lord—his own Lord, the Lord who had been crucified. Once he was certain of this, there could be no faith more complete than his.

The words that follow are not necessarily words of rebuke to him; but they are very distinctly words of challenge to all who read them. 'Because you have seen me you have found faith. Happy are they who never saw me and yet have found faith.'

6

THE RISEN CHRIST AND THE EXODUS

Come, ye faithful, raise the strain
Of triumphant gladness;
God has brought his Israel
Into joy from sadness;
Loosed from Pharaoh's bitter yoke
Jacob's sons and daughters;
Led them, with unmoistened foot,
Through the Red Sea waters.

THE hymn which begins with these words was written in Greek by St. John of Damascus in the eighth century. Translated by J. M. Neale, it has become well known to English-speaking Christians, and it forms a triumphant feature in many Eastertide services.

The first thing we notice about it, however, is that it does not begin by referring directly to our Lord's Resurrection. The first verse refers to something that had happened many centuries before. It is concerned with the Exodus—the escape of the Israelites from Egypt, across the Red Sea. What is the connection between the Exodus and Easter?

For many generations God's people had been living in Egypt as an oppressed nation, subject to forced labour. At last, under their leader Moses, they made a desperate bid for freedom. They set out all together, and succeeded in reaching the shore of the Red Sea—the narrow northern section of that sea, probably somewhere near the place where the town of Suez now stands.

From there they looked back and saw clouds of dust rapidly

approaching, which told them that the chariots and horse-men of the Egyptian army were in pursuit of them. Their position appeared to be quite hopeless. The sea was in front of them : the chariots and horsemen were closing in from behind. However, they cried to God for help, and the answer came to their leader—'Wherefore criest thou unto me? Speak to the children of Israel that they go forward.' (Exod. 14 : 15.)

That night a mighty strong east wind blew, driving back the sea-waters. People who live near a sea-coast will know by experience how an exceptional wind, blowing in a certain direction, can drive the sea-waters up a river-bed and cause flooding far inland at high tide. This wind drove the waves back from that part of the sea-bed which the Israelites had reached, so that the water became shallow enough for them to cross. By morning light all of them were safely across on the opposite shore.

The Egyptians set out to follow them ; but before they had gone very far their chariot-wheels sank into the soft sand of the sea-bed. With the dawn, the wind changed, bringing back the sea-waters. The Egyptians turned and tried to make their way back to safety ; but it was too late. They were overtaken by the tide.

In this great deliverance, God's people saw the action of the living God, who had intervened 'with a mighty hand and with a stretched-out arm.' The memory of it was kept alive, all down the centuries, by the yearly feast of the Passover, just as the memory of Christ's Resurrection is kept alive in Christian lands by the yearly celebration of Easter. For that matter, it is kept alive also by the weekly celebration of Sun-day, which is observed in Christian countries simply and solely because it was on the first day of the week that Christ's tomb was found empty, and that he showed himself alive to his disciples.

After the Crucifixion, these men who believed in Jesus were very much in the same position as the Israelites at the Red Sea. All they had hoped for seemed to have come irretrievably

44

to nothing. Yet a few weeks later we find these same men in the streets of Jerusalem proclaiming the news of their Master's Resurrection, no longer hiding behind locked doors for fear of the Jewish rulers, but apparently fearing no men. They were so obviously transformed, as the result of a great experience, that all who saw and heard them were impressed. They were so obviously witnessing to things that they themselves had heard and seen, that thousands believed.

Most of those people who have a share in the true Easter joy can probably look back to experiences of the power of prayer and of the sacraments in their own lives. They know the difference that belief in the risen Christ can make because they themselves have experinced it.

But even if that were not so, and even if they were like those other people (and there are many such to-day) who do not *want* to believe, Eastertide would bring them two very difficult problems to solve. The first is to account for the change that took place in these original Christian witnesses. Could anything short of the *fact* of their Master's Resurrection—a complete assurance that he is alive, and that he is the Lord of the world to come—have enabled these simple, rather timid men, to bear their witness so effectively as the results show that they did? The other problem is to account for the fact that throughout nearly three hundred years, men, women and children accepted torture and death rather than renounce their belief in the risen Christ; and still that belief continued to spread, until at last it became so strong that it had to be tolerated, although it set up (as it always must do) a rival power and a rival obedience over against the exclusive claims of the State.

Here, Christians say, is clear evidence of the action of God. We feel about it as God's ancient people felt when they looked back to the Exodus.

The Christian Religion is not concerned with what men have thought, or with what men have discovered, about God. It is concerned with what God has revealed to men. Its

45

subject-matter is the result not of men's experiments but of God's action.

How is the Exodus connected with Easter?

There have been two chief stages in the Revelation that God has made to men. The first stage was the calling of Israel, culminating in their escape from Egypt and their settlement in the Promised Land. This brought about the Religion of the Old Covenant, or Old Testament, in which God made himself known to one nation, through the Law and the Prophets. And, in spite of many failures, that one nation did succeed in keeping the light of the knowledge of the living God burning until the time of Christ.

The second stage of God's Revelation began with the Birth of Jesus and culminated in his Resurrection, and in the Descent of the Holy Spirit which followed, bringing to the human race a new Covenant, a new Testament, a new Church and people of God—no longer restricted to one nation, but thrown wide open to men and women of every nation and of every kind, freemen and slaves, rich and poor, brown and white and black.

An important question to ask ourselves at Eastertide is, 'How much does it mean to me that I belong to the community of believers?' Whatever else we think of on Easter Day, do let us give a thought to those millions of people throughout the world who are rejoicing with us in the Resurrection of our Lord. We cannot think of them without realizing how closely our belief binds us to them.

'Speak to the children of Israel that they go forward.' Those who know Christ, and the power of his Resurrection, cannot help knowing that they have a message which the whole world needs. The Easter message can never be good news merely for the individual. That bond which unites him to his fellow-believers throughout the world is closer and stronger than any other bond, whether of nationality or race or colour or political opinion or taste or training.

Many people of our time have been accustomed to think

of their religion as a private transaction between God and themselves. To-day the truth is being forced upon us more and more that such a view of the Christian Religion is a radically wrong one. There are *three* parties concerned in it —God and the Kingdom of God and the individual believer; Christ and the Church of Christ and the Christian. The Saviour lived and died and rose again to bring into existence a new people of God, a new Israel. To be a Christian is, first of all, to be a member of that community, and our member-ship of it should rank first in our thoughts. It is this world-wide community of believers that rejoices at Easter in our divine Leader's triumph over sin and death.

> *Come, ye faithful, raise the strain*
> *Of triumphant gladness;*
> *God has brought his Israel*
> *Into joy from sadness;*
> *Loosed from Pharaoh's bitter yoke*
> *Jacob's sons and daughters;*
> *Led them, with unmoistened foot,*
> *Through the Red Sea waters.*

'Pharaoh's bitter yoke' is the bondage into which we were born—condemned to serve the purposes of the World, the Flesh and the Devil. You have only to listen to the radio, or to watch television, or to read the newspapers, to realize how powerful the World, the Flesh and the Devil are in England to-day, and how many millions of minds and lives they are holding in slavery. Belief in the risen Christ can set us free from that hard bondage.

The powers of Evil had done their worst when they had stripped him, and nailed him to a cross, and mocked him, and watched him until he died. There was nothing more that they could do. It looked like the end; and to the world it still looks like the end.

But when he came back to his disciples, on the first Easter

47

Day, they realized that it was the Powers of Evil that had been defeated. God had intervened once more, 'with a mighty hand and with a stretched-out arm.' The Leader had gained the victory not only for himself, but for all who believe in him. He had led a new people of God 'through the Red Sea waters' into a state of freedom. And the message was for all. Repentance and remission of sins were to be proclaimed in his name among all nations. (St. Luke 24 : 47.)

Since then, how many millions have believed in the risen Christ and, believing, have shared his victory!

7

THE RISEN CHRIST AND THE FUTURE LIFE

WE hear a good deal about the instincts which cause animals and birds to act in certain ways. Many of these instincts are very remarkable, and quite beyond our power to explain. For instance, there is the instinct which can guide a pair of swallows over hundreds of miles of land and sea and bring them back to the very same spot in England where they had their nest last summer. Instinct is usually a sure guide.

And instincts play their part in the lives of men and women. One of the strongest of these is the *immortality-instinct*—a deep conviction that our conscious existence is not necessarily tied to the life of a material body, but that it continues after the body has been discarded. This sense of immortality is found among men of all races, and in all parts of the world. The evidence of inscriptions, monuments and prehistoric burial places shows that it has existed right back through the ages, as far as any facts about human life can be traced with any great degree of certainty.

But in the present age there are many people who think they cannot hold this belief in a future life because, as they would say, it is not a *scientific* belief. That is rather like saying that they cannot believe that there is any such thing as music, because music cannot be weighed or measured or analysed scientifically. Science is concerned only with facts which can be tested and proved by experiments, the kind of experiments which can be repeated and which will always give the same result. There are many things in life, however, which cannot be submitted to that kind of test. None the less,

D

they are perfectly real, and some of them are very important.

When people lose their belief in the life after death they react in various ways. Some try to find compensation in a belief about *this* world which they assume to be the only real world. They think that nothing can be real unless it makes itself known to us through our present five bodily senses. So they turn to a belief in the future of this world which they can cling to, as the next best thing to belief in a life after death.

Fifty years ago people who followed this line of thought were saying that life in this world would soon become so wonderful, and so long, that it would fully satisfy all the needs of man's nature. After half a century there seem to be few signs that things actually are working out in that way, and perhaps rather more signs that the opposite is likely to happen. Yet in spite of the history of the past fifty years, and the state of the world to-day, many still think that they ought to cling to that opinion—that belief in Man must take the place of belief in God, and that some kind of Heaven-on-earth will take the place of the real Heaven.

Others try to think of themselves as destined to live on in this world in the persons of their children and grandchildren. But they must know, if they ever analyse that idea, that it is a fallacy. No part of our own conscious being is in our children. Their lives, their souls, are completely distinct from our own.

Neither of these ideas can satisfy the *immortality-instinct*. So some people (and their number seems to be continually increasing) spend their lives in trying to escape from it. They are people who dislike being alone. They dare not allow themselves to think about the deeper aspects of life and death. They dread being reminded of the fact that they cannot go on living in this world for ever. So they spend their time in a whirl of superficial activity—rushing about from place to place, watching shadows move across a screen—anything that can help them to escape from reality. Such people deserve our sympathy and need our prayers. But we would be very sorry if we thought we would ever have to imitate them. What a poor version of a man's life it must be!

Others go to the opposite extreme. They turn to Spiritualism, and try to get into communication with their departed relatives and friends. And some of them claim that in this way they get evidence of survival which puts the matter beyond doubt.

It may be so. Christian believers see no reason to become excited about such statements. They have always realized that separation from the body does not mean the end of a man's existence. In fact their lives have been influenced and guided, all through the years, by that conviction. If they had not held it they would have lived differently.

The methods used by Spiritualists seem to us at best dangerous, and at worst deceptive. Departed souls are not the only spiritual beings who exist, and not all spiritual agencies are good, or to be trusted. There are warnings in the Bible against dabbling in necromancy; but in any case we cannot see any reason why we should wish to resort to these doubtful and dangerous methods.

It can be claimed that even common sense itself bears witness to the fact that the life of a man is something more than the life of his body. Those who have seen a friend or relative die do not need to be told that the dead body is not the person they knew so well, but merely a discarded garment—a means of self-expression which that person can no longer use. Common sense teaches people to say, at that moment, 'he is gone,' and to feel that those words express the truth of what has happened.

But Christian believers have a much clearer light on the subject than this. 'Our Saviour Jesus Christ has broken the power of death and brought life and immortality to light through the Gospel.' (2 Tim. 1 : 10.) He has shown us what a man's true life is—the kind of life that begins here and continues after the body of flesh and blood has been laid aside. This life, which cannot be destroyed by physical death, is shown to us most plainly in his own life and his own teachings. But it also appears in his dealings with his Church throughout nineteen centuries, in the witness of all his saints and of countless numbers of other good Christian men and women. At a lower level it has been shown to us in our own experience of grace and forgiveness, our experience of God's fatherly care for us through the years, our experiences of communion with God. Though these may have been only slight and fleeting glimpses, we can still recognize that these moments have been the best in our lives. Any matter-of-fact Churchman, who worships God, whose prayers are alive, and who makes a right use of the sacraments, can say 'Amen' to these words. 'Our Saviour Jesus Christ has broken the power of death and brought life and immortality to light.'

The Christian Faith meets our deepest needs. It meets our needs because it is a system of truths which have been revealed by God. They have been revealed by God because, although we need to know them and they are indeed essential for the well-being of the human race, they lie beyond the reach of Man's discovery.

What is it that is hindering people, at this moment, from accepting this, except a feeling that they ought to believe that Man is almighty and omniscient?

Revealed truth connects the future life with a resurrection of the body. Jesus did not merely survive death. He *rose from the dead*. The first Christians had to reckon not only with the fact that he appeared to them and showed himself alive, but also with the fact that his tomb was empty.

This does not mean that in other cases the resurrection body will be composed of the same particles of matter that were put into the ground. The particles of matter of which our bodies are composed are continually changing. Yet they are still our own bodies, as they were ten years ago, or forty or sixty years ago, if we were alive at that date.

It is a familiar fact that our body-forming identity continues through all the changes of the material particles. It is a part of the Easter message that this body-forming identity continues also after the body of flesh and blood has been discarded. At the proper time it will gather to itself its own body—a 'spiritual body,' the New Testament calls it, for 'flesh and blood can never possess the kingdom of God.' (1 Cor. 15 : 50.)

There is need for great caution in arguing by analogy from the risen Body of Christ. His Resurrection was a unique happening, as he is a unique Person. None the less, Christians have realized from the first that their Lord's Resurrection has something to tell them about their own future destiny. He is 'the first-born from the dead' (Rev. 1 : 5), 'the eldest among a large family of brothers.' (Rom. 8 : 29.)

It implies that those who belong to him—or, to use his own phrase, 'those who have been judged worthy of a place in the other world and of the resurrection from the dead' (Luke 20 : 35)—will one day be like him. They will share in the conditions of his risen, or rather of his ascended, life. The Prayer Book means nothing less than this when it speaks of 'our perfect consummation and bliss, both in body and soul,' and of our being 'partakers of everlasting glory in the life to come.'

8

THE RISEN CHRIST AND THE CHURCH'S MISSION

In spite of all their rejoicing in the fact of his Resurrection, the appearances of the risen Christ to his disciples must have been experiences which they half longed for and half feared. He was their dearly-loved Master. But still they could not forget that he came to them from beyond the veil of death. He came, in fact, as the conqueror of death, the Lord of both worlds.

This knowledge (even if there had been nothing else) must have caused an overmastering sense of awe, although he did all that could be done to lessen their fears and to convince them that his visits to them were as real, and as matter-of-fact, as the other events of their lives. Perhaps this was the reason why he came, on some occasions, when they were least expecting him and in a way which seemed so natural that recognition was gradual rather than immediate.

An example of this is his appearance, early one morning, on the shore of the Sea of Tiberias (John 21 : 1), the scene of many memories which he shared with them. 'The Sea of Tiberias' is, of course, only an alternative name for the Sea of Galilee. Tiberias was a fair-sized town on the western shore.

The disciples had returned to this familiar scene after their weeks of intense emotional strain in Jerusalem. It should be borne in mind that these men were neither philosophers nor mystics. They were plain, practical men, hard to convince, slow to believe, slower still to understand. They knew by this time, beyond any possibility of doubt, that their Master had risen. Obviously then, life could never be the same for them again. They had received a commission which implied that their future was going to be altogether new and strange.

But for the present they were back in their old haunts, and the Master was not with them—or so it seemed. For several days nothing unusual had happened. It was quite natural that during this interval they should have felt a longing for their old occupation and for the skills of their craft.

So one evening, as the fishing boats were putting out to sea, Peter suddenly said 'I'm going fishing.' The other six men who were with him answered at once 'We are coming too.' So Peter, James and John, Thomas and Nathanael, and two others who are not named, put out for a night's fishing.

They fished all through the night without a single catch. There was nothing very remarkable in that. It was a thing that had happened to them before. All the same it was disappointing. As the dawn began to break, seven weary and rather disheartened men pulled the boat in toward the shore.

When they were about a hundred yards from land a voice hailed them. Through the dim morning light they could see someone standing on the beach. The Stranger asked 'Have you caught anything, lads?' 'No!' they shouted back. And he told them 'Shoot the net to starboard, and you will make a catch.' A man standing on the beach might be able to see some signs of a shoal of fish which could not be seen from the boat. In any case, there would be no harm in trying once more.

So they let down the net over the right side of the boat, as they had been advised, and soon found it so full of fish that they were not strong enough to draw it back into the boat again. Amid the excitement which followed, John whispered to Peter, 'It is the Lord.'

Probably the last thing they would have expected just then was a visit from their risen Master, or that he would come just in this way. But John had remembered a similar happening in the past. (Luke 5 : 1–11.) On that occasion too they had toiled all night and caught no fish. And on that occasion, although broad daylight had come and the beach had been crowded with people, the Master had told them to put out a little way from the shore and let down the net; and when they did so they found it full.

It was no uncommon thing to meet with a shoal of fish, even close to the shore. Consequently it had been some moments before they realized how significant it was that this had happened just when and how it did. In fact, it was only when the nets began to break and the boats to sink down under the weight of fish that the truth had flashed upon Peter, and he knelt before Jesus with the cry, 'Go. Lord, leave me, sinner that I am!' And Jesus had answered 'Do not be afraid; from now on you will be catching men.'

It would be clear to the Apostles that this later incident had the same meaning as the earlier one. But on this occasion, although there were so many fish, it is recorded that 'the net was *not* torn.' The Saviour had died and was risen. Soon, in the outpouring of the Holy Spirit on the first Whitsunday, the Holy Catholic Church was to be born and the New Testament era to begin.

The meaning of this incident should be as clear to Christians of every age as it was to the first disciples. The risen Lord works through men and women who believe in him. He stands on the shore, longing to help and save the millions of our own time who have great need of him. Since his crucifixion and resurrection he can do nothing else, without human co-operation, except to stand on the shore. But it is only by his power, by contact with him, by obedience to his commands, that the net can be filled. There are, for instance, the people whom we ourselves know and meet. The risen Master wants them to become members of his Kingdom, but they will not be won unless we let him use us for the purpose, or until he can find others who will act where we have failed.

Although John was the first to recognize, Peter was the first to act. As soon as he heard those words 'It is the Lord,' he put on his fisherman's coat and plunged into the sea, swimming and wading to the shore. The others followed in the boat, dragging the laden net after them. Being fishermen, they naturally counted that record catch, and it is equally natural that they should have remembered the number of fish—a hundred and fifty-three.

When they reached the shore they saw a charcoal fire burning there, with fish placed on it, and bread. The Master invited them to make their contribution to the meal which he was preparing for them. 'Bring some of the fish that you have caught,' he said. And then, when the fish were cooked, 'Come and have breakfast.'

Although this was not a eucharistic meal, it seems right to notice at this point that we have to make our contribution before the wonder of the Eucharist can take place. It is our own offering of bread and wine which the risen Christ consecrates, so that they may be the means by which he admits us to his human Presence and feeds us with his own life. He could not come to us in Holy Communion unless we provided the bread and the wine.

What a Biblical critic makes of the account of this particular appearance of the risen Christ will inevitably depend, to some extent, on the presuppositions with which he approaches it. On the mind of the Christian believer it will probably make two strong impressions. The first is, that this is hardly the kind of scene that would have been imagined or invented by a maker of myths, with the object of portraying Jesus as some kind of demi-god. He could have done better for his purpose than this, we feel. And the second is, that in spite of its post-Resurrection strangeness, the whole scene is thoroughly characteristic of the Jesus of the Gospels. Here we have Jesus himself, homely, caring for ordinary human needs, not giving a display of supernatural splendour or bringing new information about the life beyond death, but preparing a meal for cold and hungry men; saying simply 'Bring some the fish that you have caught,' and later, 'Come and have breakfast'; and yet making an unlimited claim for allegiance.

The coat which Peter had flung round him before he plunged into the sea would need to be dried. It does not seem unduly fanciful to conclude that Jesus himself helped him to put it on again, that Peter was unwilling that he should do so, and that there is an allusion to this in the words spoken to Peter after the meal was over—'When you were young you used to dress yourself and go where you liked; but when you are an old man, you are going to stretch out your hands and someone else will dress you and take you where you do not want to go.' (v. 18; J.B.P.)

There is one brief and apparently quite artless statement in this account which seems specially worthy of notice. 'None of the disciples dared to ask "Who are you?" They knew it was the Lord.' Those few words convey to us, better than many words could do, both the fact that the Lord's appearance was changed and the sense of instinctive awe—the dread of the supernatural—which was in the minds of the disciples.

This has a meaning for us communicants of to-day. In Holy Communion there is the same mystery, the same merging of this world with another. And in every good communion there will be something of the same sense of awe in the mind of the communicant, however often he receives and however familiar he becomes with the act of receiving. 'They knew it was the Lord.'

In Holy Communion we receive life from God. One might suppose that is a gift to which nothing could be added. Yet in a sense we are continually receiving life from God. Our very existence, from moment to moment, depends on that. God is the Source of all life.

But the life which is given in Holy Communion is also a human life, and it is a life which comes to us from beyond the barriers of death—a life which has passed through death and conquered it. In Holy Communion we receive the risen Christ, who was dead and is alive for ever. (Rev. 1 : 18.)

The dialogue between the risen Lord and Peter, which forms the last scene in this last chapter of St. John's Gospel, is a thing of such poignant beauty that one feels inclined to leave it to speak for itself, lest any attempt at comment should lessen the effect. Yet it seems right to point out how the passage completes the teaching given in this appearance of the risen Christ.

The Apostles were entrusted with a twofold task—to bring souls into the Church and to feed the souls that are in the Church. For the first part of this task they were to be fishers of men; for the second, they were to be shepherds of Christ's flock.

Every Church member has a duty to gain new Church members. No one can really believe in the divine Saviour without wishing to bring others to him. It is hard to imagine any first-century Christian missing a chance to gain a convert. But the New Testament makes it clear that it was the Apostles themselves who took the lead in this evangelistic work.

The New Testament writings show that these first leaders of the Church did not think of themselves merely as men who were bound in conscience to bear witness to a remarkable event, of which they had first-hand knowledge. They reveal in these men a compelling sense of their responsibility as commissioned messengers of the one Saviour, heralds of a new era, fully-accredited ambassadors of the Kingdom of God.

The laity can share in the Church's pastoral work too, and many do so, as sick visitors, Sunday School teachers, leaders of youth groups—not to mention Readers, who at the present time rank as laymen.

But it was to bishops and priests especially, through Peter, that Christ said 'Feed my sheep.' The pastoral care of Church members belonged directly to the Apostles and to the men whom they ordained. Every epistle in the New Testament is a pastoral epistle. Every priest is commissioned to dispense God's Word and sacraments, and these are as necessary to the life of the Christian soul as food is to the body.

In this dialogue the Lord commissions Peter as a Chief

Pastor of the Church. He did not single out Peter from the rest merely as one who had a special need of forgiveness. He had already appeared to him separately, soon after his Resurrection (Luke 24 : 34; 1 Cor. 15 : 5), and in that appearance all Peter's doubts as to his forgiveness must have been set at rest.

According to St. Mark's Gospel, the angel had singled out Peter in the message given to the women. 'Go and give this message to his disciples *and Peter.*' (Mark 16 : 7.) For that matter, the Lord himself had singled him out in words spoken just before he left the Upper Room for Gethsemane. 'Simon, Simon, take heed : Satan has been given leave to sift all of you like wheat : but for you' (that is, for Peter specially) 'I have prayed that your faith may not fail; and when you have come to yourself, you must lend strength to your brothers.' (Luke 22 : 31, 32.)

After the meal, then, Jesus leads Peter a little distance away from the rest (John 21 : 20) to give him this charge.[1] 'Simon, son of John, do you love me more than they do?' 'Yes, Lord,' he answered, 'you know I am your friend.' 'Then feed my lambs,' he said. A second time he asked, 'Simon, son of John, do you love me?' 'Yes, Lord, you know I am your friend.' 'Then tend my sheep.' A third time he said, 'Simon, son of John, are you my friend?' Peter was hurt that at the third asking he should have said 'Are you my friend?' 'Lord,' he said, 'you know everything. You know I am your friend.' Jesus said 'Feed my sheep.'

[1] I am following the alternative translation which the New English Bible gives in footnotes. It seems hard to understand why the Greek text should ring the changes on two different words for 'love' if the difference has no particular significance.

9

THE RISEN CHRIST IN THE CHRISTIAN

MANY things that are written in the Bible have come to mean much less to us, in actual fact, than they ought to mean, chiefly I think because we have become so familiar with them. We cannot remember when we heard the words for the first time; and we certainly could not count the number of times we have heard them. One of the advantages of reading the New Testament in a modern translation is that it sets us free, to some extent, from the deadening effect of over-familiarity. It makes it more possible for us to receive the message freshly, almost as though we had never heard it before.

Let us try to look in this way, for example, at a single verse —2 Corinthians 5 : 17. 'When any one is united to Christ, there is a new world : the old order has gone, and a new order has already begun.' This verse says something which is obviously important. And it immediately raises the question, 'How does one become united to Christ?'

In the first place, by sharing in the life of the believing and worshipping Christian community. The New Testament associates the Church very closely indeed with the risen Christ. It is through his Church that he still teaches and acts and prays in this world. (Rom. 12 : 4 ,5; 1 Cor. 12 : 12–26; Ephes. 4 : 11–16; Col. 1 : 18, 24; Matthew 18 : 17–20; John 15 : 1–6).[1]

But when the New Testament speaks of a Christian being united to Christ it means something more than that he is an active Church member. It means that he is in touch with God

[1] Cf. also St. Ignatius, Ephesians 5 : 'I congratulate you, who are knit to him as closely as is the Church to Jesus Christ and Jesus Christ to the Father.'

through Christ in such a way that this influence controls and shapes his life so that he is, to all intents and purposes, living in a new world.

It is what the Master himself promised. 'I have come that men may have life, and may have it in all its fulness.' (John 10 : 10.) 'Whoever comes to me shall never be hungry, and whoever believes in me shall never be thirsty.' (John 6 : 35.) The New Testament was written in days when this experience was quite new and fresh, both to the men who wrote about it and to their readers. They had never met with anything like it until they became Christians. It transformed their lives. It changed their ways of thinking, their standards of value, their motives, their characters. And they could not mistake the fact that this influence reached them from the risen Christ.

It was from a knowledge of Christ as a risen Lord and Saviour, a personal experience of his power through their fellowship in the Church, that the first Christians looked back on his Resurrection and Crucifixion and, beyond that, on his short earthly life. The Christian life cannot have changed its nature. It is with this knowledge that the twentieth-century believer must begin, and to the ripening of this personal experience that all the practice of his religion should tend.

If we are to know Jesus we must seek to know him as he is, that is, we must seek to know him as risen and ascended. Belief in a dead Christ is an unreality. There have been some in our time who have been content to think of him merely as a Teacher who lived long ago, whose life was so perfect that we can safely accept it as a pattern and find in it a revelation of God. But such a belief cannot bring any one to a true knowledge of Christ.

He is not to be found in the Gospel records, though our search for him may begin there. By showing him to us as he was, these records are intended to help us to know him as he is. When a Christian says 'The third day he rose again from the dead,' he is doing something far more vital than expressing an opinion about an alleged event in the past. He is expressing the Faith which he submits to the test of everyday prayer and everyday life, and which he finds by experience to be true. When he says those words it is as though he were laying his hand for a moment against the main pillar of the temple of God in which his life is lived. To live a Christian life is to 'grow in grace and in the knowledge of our Lord and Saviour Jesus Christ.' (2 Peter 3 : 18.)

Now let us be clear about this. When Christians say that they know Christ, they mean something that is quite real and practical. They are not thinking of visions and voices and experiences which belong to an advanced stage of mystical progress, but of a knowledge which all can share. There are other ways of knowing, beside seeing and weighing and measuring. In fact it is not by seeing and weighing and measuring, but in totally different ways, that we really get to know a living person.

The knowledge of Christ grows in the Christian through the practices of our religion—through prayer and the sacraments, through corporate worship and private meditation, and through trying to keep our thoughts in touch with him among all the business of everyday life. It may grow more quickly or more slowly, according to the degree of sincerity with which these means of grace are used. But in any case our knowledge becomes much clearer when we realize this simple truth, that all the special help and strength and guidance which we gain from these practices come to us from the divine and human Person whom we are seeking to know, who can be known because he is living, and who is living because he rose from the dead.

I can remember a time when this fact came home to my mind almost with the force of a revelation. I wondered why Christian preachers and teachers had not pointed it out to me before. Probably they had, but somehow or other I had managed to miss it. I had been waiting and hoping for something different. When I look back it seems to me that I had been led to expect some kind of exceptional religious experience. But normally, men come to know Jesus Christ, and to recognize him, simply through the grace that he gives. That grace is unmistakably real, and it leads to a knowledge of the Person who gives it which is also unmistakably real.

People are sometimes given the impression that a personal knowledge of Christ can be gained only by an abnormal experience of conversion, an emotional crisis which will bring a moment of illumination. Nothing of that kind is promised, nor is it necessary. We know that such things have happened, and that they have marked a turning point in the lives of some very noteworthy Christians. But they are exceptions.

Most Christians come to know Christ in a perfectly plain and normal way through his influence in their lives. They pray to him and find that he helps them. They go to him for forgiveness and know that they are forgiven. They obey his command to receive Holy Communion, and find that his life does enter into them and grow in them more and more. All this adds up to something that is quite real, though it cannot be seen or weighed or measured. Once we have gained it, we could never be willing to live without it.

Let us look a little more in detail at these ways in which the Christian believer gains a personal knowledge of the risen Christ.

First there is prayer. Christian prayer is usually prayer addressed to God the Father, through the Son, in the unity of the Holy Spirit; but it can be, and often is, addressed directly to Christ as God. The Litany, for instance, is addressed directly to the risen and ascended Christ. Any one who will read the words attentively, from 'whom thou hast redeemed with thy most precious blood' to 'O Christ, hear us,' will see that this is so, although it may be true that many Church-people lose sight of this fact when they are actually saying the Litany. There are probably few Christians who do not at times pray directly to our Lord Jesus Christ.

This prayer is found, in Christian experience, to be true conversation. It is a road where there is two-way traffic. 'He who loves me will be loved by my Father; and I will love him and disclose myself to him.' (John 14: 21.) The response comes, though it may not be the response which was expected nor come in the way that was expected. We turn to Christ for counsel as we would to a friend, and for direction as we would to a leader; and he, in reply, 'puts into our minds good desires,' practical guidance, an insight into our own mistakes and the ways in which they can be corrected. An important element in Christian prayer is to train ourselves to be receptive and attentive, whether the guidance comes during the time of prayer or at other times. It comes, perhaps, more often after the time of prayer is over. It grows up in our thoughts so naturally that we may scarcely notice it, or recognize it for what it is. Yet every Christian knows that in this way prayer makes a real difference to him, enabling Christ to influence his life and enabling him to grow in the knowledge of Christ.

But selfishness is a hindrance to friendship, and prayer which is merely self-regarding or merely formal cannot, in the nature of things, lead to a personal knowledge of Christ. 'I saw two conditions needful in them that pray, according to that I have felt in myself,' wrote Lady Julian of Norwich. (*Comfortable Words for Christ's Lovers,* ch. 19.) 'One is, that they will not pray for anything that may be, but that thing that is God's will and his worship. Another is that they set them mightily and continually to beseech that thing that is his will and his worship.'

At this point some readers may be helped by a reminder that thoughts can pass from one person to another without the use of any outward means of communication. It has been proved, by many experiments, that it is possible for some persons, at least, to transmit their thoughts directly to others by the process called 'telepathy'; and when this takes place the distance between the persons concerned seems to make no difference to the result. This is mentioned not, of course, as an exact parallel but merely as an analogy. We may be very firmly convinced that we can make contact with the risen Christ through prayer. But even when an experience seems unmistakably real, we feel more satisfied about it when we have found some kind of answer to the question, 'How can it happen?'

Then there is the experience of forgiveness through Christ. Whether this is gained in prayer or through the sacrament of Penance, it has brought to countless numbers of men and women an unforgettable and unexpected sense of having been set at peace with God and with men. The burden of the past is lifted and life begins afresh. This experience, to which Christians have witnessed throughout the world and throughout the centuries, must be accepted as evidence of the power of the risen Christ, who even during his earthly life claimed to have the right to forgive sins. (Luke 5 : 18–26.)

There is the evidence of Holy Communion. 'He that eats my flesh and drinks my blood dwells continually in me and I in him.' (John 6 : 56.) It was characteristic of our Lord to give us this Gift under the simple, homely forms of bread and wine. It was characteristic of him, too, to speak of it in terms which compel a decision, whether it is to 'withdraw and no longer go about with him' or to say 'Your words are words of eternal life.' (John 6 : 66–9.)

'The last Adam has become a life-giving spirit,' wrote St. Paul. (1 Cor. 15 : 45.) It is as a life-giving spirit that the Christian has experience of Christ in Holy Communion. And what is true of Holy Communion and of Penance is equally true of the other sacraments. They are not memorials of a dead Master, but means of contact with the risen Christ, which convey healing, light and strength into the spiritual nature of all who receive them worthily.

Earlier in this chapter there is the statement that the living Christ is not to be found in the Gospels. It is none the less true that it is possible to make contact with him by reading the Gospels in a certain way, that is, with the expectation that he will use the printed words as a means of speaking to us. For the words recorded in the Gospels were spoken for us, not only for those men who happened to be living at that time. His words are different from other men's not only because of the inexhaustible store of divine and human wisdom which they contain, but also because of what they tell us about the Speaker. We find in them, either explicitly stated or implied, the claim that the most important issue in life, for all men of all kinds, is that they should not merely believe these words but also believe in the Man who spoke them.

It is this claim which gives the sayings of Jesus their unique character. As we read them, it becomes clear that they were not intended only for the little groups of people who were present in the places where they were first spoken. He was thinking of us and of those who will come after us. He was looking into the future and into the whole future to the end of time. So we read the Gospels not to learn what a dead Christ said to other men nineteen hundred years ago, but to hear what the living Christ is saying to us now. This method of Gospel-reading is the essence of the practice called 'meditation,' which has played a great part in Christian life and experience, and which most of the masters of the spiritual life commend as a necessity for all who wish to make progress.

Finally, we can learn to know the living Christ in our fellow-Christians. The lives of the saints and other outstanding Christian witnesses of the past form a very solid and weighty mass of evidence ; and the world cannot get rid of this evidence merely by ignoring it. Although the ways of thinking which are accepted by the majority of people in our own time cannot account for these lives, they demand an explanation. These men and women were convinced that they had nothing of their own except their sins, and that any good they managed to do must be attributed wholly to Jesus Christ. They are remarkable for their diversity and yet show an unmistakable family likeness. Their lives will speak for themselves to all who are willing to listen.

But in addition to these outstanding examples from the

past, most believers will agree that their own faith is strengthened by the memory of some good Christians whom they have actually known. We can find nothing in the natural order which could fully account for their lives and characters, as we knew them, and nothing else in the world which shows such clear signs of an influence from beyond this world.

It seems that all this is as it was intended to be. 'You are a light for all the world. A town that stands on a hill cannot be hidden.' (Matthew 5 : 14.) The risen Christ lives, to some extent, in every man or woman who sincerely believes in him, and his influence will show itself. In one we may recognize traces of the Master's wide sympathy ; in another, his sincerity and humility ; in another, something of his zeal for the honour of God ; in another, a grasp of spiritual realities which the world of nature cannot supply. His gifts of grace are as richly varied as his gifts in the world of nature. In every faithful Christian we can recognize some feature of character which he owes to Christ and which has grown up within him through his relationship with the risen Saviour.

When we find that a Man who died nineteen hundred years ago is still powerfully influencing the lives of large numbers of people, with an influence which they themselves know as living and personal, it becomes evident that the Man in question did not remain dead.

10

THE RISEN CHRIST AND CHRISTIAN BAPTISM

In the first Epistle of Peter, Christian Baptism is directly linked with the Resurrection of Jesus. 'Baptism . . . brings salvation through the resurrection of Jesus Christ.' (1 Peter 3 : 21.) The connection is not a difficult one to grasp. All the grace which any Christian receives through faith and prayer and the sacraments is, in fact, a sharing in the life of the risen Christ, that new life which he brought into this world for our salvation. 'I have come that men may have life, and may have it in all its fulness.' (John 10 : 10.) His death and resurrection set this life free, to be given to others; and because his human Nature is united to the Nature of God, the supply can never be exhausted. It is for all who will receive it.

In the usual course of things, a Christian's first contact with the new life that is given through Christ takes place at his baptism. The Apostles themselves, who pointed to their Master's Resurrection as a convincing proof of his power to make this gift, connected it closely with Baptism. Once a man had expressed his belief in the saving power of Christ, the first step for him to take was to be baptized. When the people in the streets of Jerusalem asked 'What are we to do?', Peter answered at once, 'Repent and be baptized every one of you, in the Name of Jesus the Messiah for the forgiveness of your sins, and you will receive the gift of the Holy Spirit.' (Acts 2 : 37, 38.) When the officer in charge of the prison at Philippi asked Paul and Silas 'What must I do to be saved?', they answered, 'Put your trust in the Lord Jesus, and you will be saved, you and your household.' 'Then they spoke the word of the Lord to him and to every one in his house. At that late hour of the night he took them and washed their wounds; and immediately afterwards he and his whole family were baptized.' (Acts 16 : 31–3.)

It was quite natural, then, for a New Testament writer to say 'Baptism brings salvation through the resurrection of Jesus Christ.' In the days of the early Church, Easter Even was the occasion when the largest number of converts were baptized,[1] and this connection has lived on through the centuries in the traditional ceremony of the blessing of the font. It appears in our own Prayer Book in the collect and epistle for Easter Even, both of which refer to Baptism.

Our own baptism, then, should never be thought of as a transaction which is over and done with. It brought us into a relationship with the risen Christ which continues throughout life and, indeed, after this earthly life is over. We have been made members of Christ in the original sense of the word 'member'—that is, a living part of a living body. It was God who took the first step, as only he could do, in setting up this relationship. Our baptism was essentially an operation which God performed in the depths of our being, through the merits of the Saviour.

But Baptism is like all the other sacraments in this respect, that the actual effects of it in the life of the person who receives it will depend on his response and co-operation. The Catechism emphasizes the truth that repentance and faith are 'required of persons to be baptized,' and that the infant children of Christian parents are baptized only on condition that their sponsors promise for them that they themselves will make this response to the grace of the sacrament when they

---

[1] Tertullian, *De Baptismo*, 19. 'The more solemn day for Baptism is afforded by the Pasch, since then indeed the passion of the Lord into which we are baptized has been completed.' But he adds, 'Every time is suitable for Baptism: if there is a difference in the festival, it makes no difference in the grace.'

are old enough to understand what has been done for them. As St. Augustine points out, when infants are baptized the sacrament of regeneration comes first; but if they keep to the Christian way of life, conversion of the mind and heart will follow. (*De Bapt. c. Don.* IV, 31.)

Churchpeople do not believe in magic. The power of God is in the sacraments, but in practice they help us only so far as we appropriate and use the gifts which they convey. There was no magic in our Lord's works of healing in the Gospel days; but the power of God was in them. 'Power went out from him' (Luke 8 : 46), but it could heal only those who made the response of faith. There were two factors in each work of healing—the power of God conveyed through contact with the Humanity of Christ, and the faith of the person healed. Their faith healed them only in the sense that it enabled the divine power to work in them.

This applies equally to the sacraments. They convey the gifts of God's grace through the risen Humanity of Christ; but those gifts become effective only so far as they are realized and welcomed and used. Provided this response is made, the daily life of the baptized Christian is, in fact and not merely in metaphor, inspired and directed by the risen Christ himself. 'Baptized into union with him, you have all put on Christ as a garment.' (Gal. 3 : 27.)

Now it is impossible for any one to live the *risen* life until he has died. Our Lord himself could not do so, nor can any disciple of his hope to do so. In thinking about the Resurrection of Jesus we have to guard against the mistake of disconnecting it from his Death. It was the crucified Christ who rose from the dead, and it was by showing the marks of the wounds in hands and feet and side that he proved his identity to his disciples. He himself had spoken of his own sufferings and death as a baptism. 'Can you drink of the cup that I drink, or be baptized with the baptism I am baptized with?' (Mark 10 : 38.) 'I have a baptism to undergo, and how hampered I am until the ordeal is over!' (Luke 12 : 50.)

Baptism brought our lives into connection with the life of the risen Christ—that is to say, of the Christ who 'was crucified, dead and buried.' 'Have you forgotten that when we were baptized into union with Christ Jesus we were baptized into his death? By baptism we were buried with him, and lay dead, in order that, as Christ was raised from the dead in the splendour of the Father, so also we might set our feet upon the new path of life. For if we have become incorporate with him in a death like his, we shall also be one with him in a resurrection like his. We know that the man we once were has been crucified with Christ, for the destruction of the sinful self, so that we may no longer be the slaves of sin.' (Rom. 6 : 3–6.) How should these words apply to the life of the average twentieth-century Christian, in those parts of the world where the Church is still free from persecution?

Philippians 3 : 10 is a verse which is sometimes incompletely quoted. 'That I may know him, and the power of his resurrection'—those words supply us with an exhilarating message for Easter and an inspiring objective for the rest of the year. But we cannot stop at that point, for it obviously would not do to edit the message of Easter to suit our own inclinations. After 'the power of his resurrection,' the verse ends with the words 'and the fellowship of his sufferings, being made conformable unto his death.' In the New English Bible the complete verse appears as follows : 'All I care for is to know Christ, to experience the power of his resurrection, and to share his sufferings, in growing conformity with his death.'

Conformity with Christ's death, then, is inseparably connected with the power of his resurrection, both in the grace conferred by baptism and in the actual living of the Christian life. Our Lord himself pointed this out very clearly. 'If any one wishes to be a follower of mine, he must leave self behind; day after day he must take up his cross, and come with me.' (Luke 9 : 23.) And again, 'No one who does not carry his cross and come with me can be a disciple of mine.' (Luke 14 : 27.) Now crosses were not in those days carried merely as burdens, or as symbols of affliction bravely borne. The cross was an instrument of shameful death, and it was carried only to the place of execution. What our Lord's saying really implies, then, is expressed by St. Paul in the words 'Every day I die.' (1 Cor. 15 : 31.)

No one can be a believing Christian in the twentieth century any more than he could in the first century unless he is willing to think for himself. It means cutting oneself adrift from those conventioned ideas of our own time which are still ruling the world, although the logic of history has shattered them.

Some years ago I saw in an evening paper the statement that 'modern people believe that the purpose of our lives is that we should express ourselves by having a good time.' There is nothing specifically modern in the idea of making pleasure the sole purpose of life. It has been tried many times in the past, and found disastrous. What does seem characteristic of our age, in that sentence, is the emphasis that is given to self-expression. To express your self—that is an ideal which many people to-day do seem to accept—quite seriously and thoughtfully.

But before we set to work to express ourselves, it seems reasonable to consider whether we have the right to be satisfied with ourselves. Can we be sure that our self is worth expressing? The Christian Church, with its well-tested experience of the power of the risen Christ, offers us a much higher ambition. We are to make it our aim not to express ourselves, just as we are by nature, but to express 'the new nature of God's creating' (Ephes. 4 : 24), that is, the natural self born anew by being brought into a living relationship with Christ. Only in this way can we find our true selves. For the 'natural' life is based on a lie. We depend on God for all our powers of body, mind and spirit; and from this it follows logically that we belong to God. To live as though that were not true—to live as though we held the cause of our existence in our own hands and as though we had originated the powers and the laws by which we live—is to build our lives on a basis which is obviously false.

Most forms of theft are still considered to be wrong, and some of them are classed as crimes. But to steal *oneself* is the worst form of theft, though it is neither punished as a crime nor condemned by public opinion.

To say that it is our nature to live in this way is merely to agree that we need a Saviour—that human nature in general, and each man and woman in particular—needs to be radically changed. It is no mere backwardness, or want of teaching, but the barrier of wilful sin, which estranges us from God. This barrier is built on that tendency to put Self into the place of God which we inherit from our forefathers. It is the rebellion of the creature, dependent on God, yet living to please himself.

It was this that crucified the Saviour. The new life which comes to us from him is a life which has withstood sin even to death. Clearly, it can find room in us only so far as we die to the old nature which crucified him, and would crucify him again.

Our baptism did not destroy that old nature, though it brought us into a relationship with Christ which makes it possible for us to gain the mastery over it. 'The infection of nature doth remain, yea in them that are regenerated.' (Articles of Religion, IX.) It is like living in a house which is built partly above and partly beneath ground-level. We can choose to live in the upper stories or to live in the basement. By the grace of Baptism we are free to make the former choice; but to remain true to it implies a continual conflict against that 'evil infection' which would prefer the atmosphere of the cellars.

Hence the need for that exercise which writers on the Christian life call 'Mortification,' that is, the destroying, the doing to death, of the old nature with its wrong opinions and preferences and motives. It is true that the death of the old nature, like the new birth, must be the work of God. But God has left our wills free. We must co-operate, with a will, in his work of grace. The inner world of our thoughts must be turned upside down. More and more, the old life must be made to give place to the new, 'in growing conformity with his death.'

'To know Christ, to experience the power of his resurrection, and to share his sufferings'—as we have seen, these are bracketed together. There are some sufferings which we cannot avoid. They come to us through no choice of our own. None the less, we can accept them in such a way that they become a sharing in the sufferings of Christ. Every Christian should know how suffering, whether or mind or body, can be turned to gold by offering it to God, for his good purposes, in union with the sufferings of Christ, the only Saviour of men. 'It is now my happiness to suffer for you,' wrote St. Paul. 'This is my way of helping to complete, in my poor human flesh, the full tale of Christ's afflictions still to be endured, for the sake of his body which is the Church.' (Col. 1 : 24.) God can use the sufferings of a Christion, when they are offered to him with this intention, just as he can use his prayers or his active service.

'The mortifications that come to us without our own seeking,' said St. Francis of Sales, 'from God or from men by his divine permission, are always more precious than those which are the offspring of our own will; and we ought to look upon it as a general rule that the less there be in our actions of what is agreable to ourselves, or of our own choice, so much the more is there in them of goodness, solidity, devotion—of what is pleasing to God and profitable to our own souls.'

But in every generation there have been fervent Christians who have taken on themselves some voluntary mortifications with the object of hastening this process of the death of the old, sin-infected nature, which alone can make room for that new life which is received from the risen Christ. In doing so, they have been following the example of Christ himself, 'who for our sake fasted forty days and forty nights.' (Collect for

Lent I.) [1] They have been following the example of St. Paul, who wrote 'I bruise my own body and make it know its master.' (1 Cor. 9 : 27.) In addition, they have been keeping the rules of the Church, which are faithfully represented in our Prayer Book by the list of 'Vigils, Fasts and Days of Abstinence to be observed in the year.'

Voluntary mortifications bring their own special danger of spiritual pride, and no one who has read the Gospels will be likely to forget how deadly that particular danger can be. But Christians who are really in earnest will know how to avoid it. To destroy pride and self-will is the main object of mortification, whether it comes by way of faithful resistance to temptation or by way of self-discipline.

Tauler gives a list of five rules 'by which the Christian can know whether self-will is destroyed and transformed into the Will of God.' (*Institutions,* ch. 36.) (1) If he refuses to consent to any sin, whether great or small, not only avoiding and resisting the evil, but turning his will away from it. (2) If he finds himself disposed to practise all the virtues which God demands from him. (3) If, fearing neither sufferings nor death, he is ready to endure all things for the love of God. (4) If he renounces everything, whether corporal or spiritual, which could hinder his union with God. (5) If his object and purpose, whatever may happen, is always the honour and glory of God.

All this may seem very far removed from the thoughts of most people, and even of most Churchpeople, to-day. But it is likely that Christians of former generations would be surprised at the comfortable version of the Christian life which passes muster among us English Christians at present. It might seem to them a denial of the Faith, rather than an expression of it. In that judgment we hope they would be mistaken. Yet it is true that co-operation with the grace of Baptism implies

[1] And how else are we to understand that later occasion when his disciples 'were urging him, "Rabbi, have something to eat": but he said "I have food to eat of which you know nothing"?' (John 4 : 31, 32.)

76

a dying to the old nature, in order to make room for something better. 'To know Christ and the power of his resurrection' means also 'to share his sufferings, in growing conformity with his death.'

What is required of us is as far as possible from being a dismal or negative or defeatist attitude to life. No one could succeed in curbing such powerful instincts as pride and self-seeking and the lust for pleasure unless he finds something more satisfying to replace them. In its positive aspect, mortification is self-giving; and giving is the essence of all personal life.

God himself becomes known to us by his giving. He *gives* us 'life and breath and all else.' (Acts 17 : 25.) The Father *gave* his only-begotten Son. He *gives* the Holy Spirit also to those who ask him. The Son loved us and *gave* himself for us. He still says to us, day by day, 'This is my Body, which is *given* for you.' The Holy Spirit is the *Giver* of life. The Church began to grow when the Apostles spoke 'as the Spirit *gave* them utterance.'

Our own life is personal life, and consists in giving. We are made after God's likeness to this extent, that it is only by giving that we are able to reflect God. Therefore the power to give is the very stuff of which our life is made. To live (as opposed to merely existing) is to use, for the glory of God and the good of his creatures, those riches which have been placed at our disposal, the power of thought, the power of prayer, the power of speech, the power to do good, the power to create beauty, the power to make others happy. These talents come to us with life itself, and the one unpardonable thing to do with a talent is to hide it in the ground. (Matthew 25 : 25.)

Our baptism opens the gate to a fuller life; but we must pass through the gate, or it will have opened in vain. The best way to deny oneself is to forget oneself; and the best way to forget oneself is to be fully occupied with the will of God and the needs of men.

The collect for Easter Even would be a good prayer to use at any time as a memorial of our baptism, for it reminds us what the daily life and daily experience of a baptized Christian should be. 'Grant, O Lord, that as we are baptized into the death of thy blessed Son our Saviour Jesus Christ, so by continual mortifying our corrupt affections we may be buried with him; and through the grave and gate of death may pass to our joyful resurrection; for his merits who died and was buried and rose again for us.'

11

THE ASCENSION

SOME Christians of our time feel a difficulty in thinking about the Ascension. The New Testament accounts of it and the words of the Creed ('He ascended into heaven and sitteth at the right hand of God the Father') seem to them to imply that Heaven is somewhere in outer space, and that Christ is sitting there on an actual throne at the right hand of the Father, in a quite literal sense. If that is not how the words are explained to-day, they say, that is what the New Testament writers really meant and what the first Christians believed.

They can be reassured. No well-instructed Christian, ancient or modern, has ever thought of God the Father as 'a venerable old man with a beard, sitting above the clouds.' The real difficulty that we have to contend with here is the fact that crude anti-Christian misrepresentations of the Faith are too often accepted without question. Some of the old artists did rather unwisely attempt to portray God in that form; but neither they nor the people who saw the pictures mistook them for actual portraits of God as he really is. Christians have always understood that God is a Spirit, that he is omnipresent, and therefore that there cannot be, in any literal sense, a right hand or left hand of God. But people of former times understood, perhaps more easily than we do, that there are some truths which can be expressed most effectively by the use of symbols and of picture-language.

In this chapter, then, I shall try to find plain answers to three questions about the Ascension. What was it that happened? What did it mean? What difference does it make to us?

1. *What happened?*

There are only two accounts of the Ascension in the New Testament, both by St. Luke, though other New Testament writers refer to it as an accepted fact. One of the accounts comes at the end of St. Luke's Gospel and the other at the beginning of Acts. In the latter account we are told that this final appearance of the risen Christ to his disciples took place forty days after his Resurrection and ten days before the coming of the Holy Spirit at Pentecost.

The account in the Gospel fixes the place of this last appearance at Bethany, in the Mount of Olives. The account in Acts, without mentioning the place, gives some fragments of conversation which show that the disciples sensed the fact that some great event was about to happen, though they were far from realizing what actually lay before them. 'Lord,' they asked, 'is this the time when you are to establish once again the sovereignty of Israel?' (Acts 1 : 6.) They were still thinking of their Master in the way in which devout Jews at that time thought of the Messiah, as a mighty Leader, who would set Israel free from the rule of the Romans and make it great among the nations of the earth.

He dealt patiently with their prejudices, as we hope he will with our own. He did not tell them that his Kingdom, which is *in* this world though not *of* this world, was to spread far beyond the bounds of one chosen nation, that it was to be a Catholic or world-wide Kingdom, in which Jews and Gentiles, people of all races and of all nations, were to find free admittance and an equal brotherhood. They were to learn this later from the teaching of the Holy Spirit. And when their national and religious prejudices are taken into consideration it is wonderful that they learnt it so quickly.

All he told them at present was, 'It is not for you to know about dates or times, which the Father has set within his own control. But you will receive power when the Holy Spirit comes upon you ; and you will bear witness for me in Jerusalem, and all over Judaea and Samaria, and' (here was the hint of future things which would amaze them and live in their memories) 'away to the ends of the earth.'

The account continues, 'When he had said this, as they watched, he was lifted up, and a cloud removed him from their sight.' This does not mean that they watched their Master rising up and up into the sky until he was lost to sight among the clouds. The cloud which 'removed him from their sight' was not a rain-cloud, but the glory of the Lord. It was like the cloud which rested on Mount Sinai at the giving of the Law, and the cloud which filled the Temple when Isaiah had his vision of God.

Perhaps we can get a clearer idea of the disciples' experience at this moment of their Master's Ascension from St. Mark's account of the Transfiguration. (Mark 9 : 2 to 8.) On that occasion, the Evangelist notes, our Lord's 'clothes became dazzling white, with a whiteness no bleacher on earth could equal.' Peter made an impulsive remark, which is honestly recorded, with the explanation that 'he did not know what to say, they were so terrified. Then came a cloud which overshadowed them and a Voice came out of the cloud.' Here we get the impression that the three witnesses, completely overawed, bowed their heads and perhaps covered their eyes. 'And now suddenly,' the account continues, 'when they looked around, there was nobody to be seen but Jesus alone with themselves.'

It seems legitimate to draw the conclusion that the words 'a cloud removed him from their sight' imply a similar experience at the Ascension. Beyond that, it hardly seems safe to venture. The last scene in the earthly life of Incarnate God, like the scene of his birth, is hidden from the eyes of the world. That he is ascended is as certain as that he was born. Although the Gospels contain no detailed account of the way in which the Ascension took place, the reign of Christ is the real subject-matter of all the other New Testament writings. The disciples saw his feet lifting from the ground, which he was to tread no longer ('as they watched, he was lifted up'), his hands stretched over them in blessing (Luke 24 : 51) and then the 'cloud,' bringing an overmastering sense of the presence of the supernatural, and of the realities of another world than this.

When the cloud had passed they stood for a while 'gazing intently into the sky.' That was natural, as it is natural that a priest at the altar should lift up his eyes and his hands when he says the words 'Glory be to God on high.' It is natural that we should sometimes look upward when we pray, since we are addressing a Being who is higher than ourselves. The word 'higher,' like the word 'heaven' has two meanings and the fact that those two meanings are naturally connected in our minds does not mean that we are confusing them whenever we apply to one the symbols or gestures which belong to the other.

I was once called to the bedside of a dying man who had spent all his active life in the Regular Army. During the years that he lived in retirement, he rarely spoke about his religion, though he was never absent from church on a Sunday if he could help it. Unfortunately, I heard of his illness so late that when I reached him he was too weak even to whisper or, as it seemed, to make any movement, though he was fully conscious. When I had finished the prayers and given him the blessing, however, he *lifted up* his eyes and his hands in an unforgettable gesture of adoration. He must have summoned his last ounce of strength to do this, for he died immediately afterwards. How else could he have expressed adoration and prayer, in that last moment?

It was natural, then, that the disciples should have remained looking into the empty sky until a voice broke the spell. 'Men of Galilee, why stand there looking up into the sky? This Jesus, who has been taken from you up to heaven, will come in the same way as you have seen him go.' The 'two men in white' who 'stood beside them' belonged to the world into which their Master had passed.

2. *What did it mean?*

The day of the Ascension was the Coronation Day of Jesus, who still keeps that human nature which he took from his Mother. In ancient times, an Emperor who had given supreme power and honour to one of his subjects, would make the fact publicly known by seating him at his right hand. Hence the picture-language of the Creed—'He sitteth at the right hand of God the Father.'

'Jesus, the Saviour, reigns.' Since the day of the Ascension all that remains is the working-out in this world of what is already an established fact in the world beyond. History cannot take any other form, or have any other meaning.

It may be said that the events of our time do not seem to suggest this. But it should be remembered that we are living in an age of apostasy. This consideration does make sense of the actual state of the world to-day, which must seem inexplicable to those who cling to the idea that we are living in a time of universal progress.

Jesus reigns with the power of God, who is Love. He will never unmake men by taking away their freedom, but he will do all that Love can do to win their allegiance. It is the rule of divine patience. 'Christ offered for all time one sacrifice for sins, and took his seat at the right hand of God, where he waits henceforth until his enemies are made his footstool.' (Heb. 10 : 12, 13.) But it is also the rule of unconquerable power. 'He is destined to reign until God has put all enemies under his feet.' (1 Cor. 15 : 25.) In the first recorded preaching of the Gospel, St. Peter quotes this same 110th psalm. (Acts 2 : 35.)

The original meaning of this psalm belongs to the past, as the figure of a throned and sceptred potentate belongs to the past; but the Holy Spirit has made use of this language and this symbol to bring home to our minds the reality of the reign of Christ.

The Ascension did not mean that the Master had left his disciples. It did not bring that experience of separation and of loneliness which men feel when death robs them of one whom they love and on whom they depend. They had experienced that feeling of bereavement when his Body was in the sepulchre. They felt nothing of that kind now. 'They returned to Jerusalem with great joy.' (Luke 24 : 52.) They were men with a mission, who knew that their Leader was invincible. 'One of those who bore us company,' St. Peter told them, 'all the while we had the Lord Jesus with us, coming and going, from John's ministry of baptism until the day when he was taken up from us—one of those must now join us as a witness to his resurrection.' (Acts 1 : 21, 22.) Because their Master had been 'taken up,' they knew that he is Lord of All, and this knowledge gave them a fearlessness which impressed all who came in contact with them (Acts 4 : 13), so that the fishermen, Peter and John, could say to the High Priest and rulers of the people, 'Is it right in God's eyes for us to obey you rather than God? Judge for yourselves. We cannot possibly give up speaking of things we have seen and heard.' (Acts 4 : 19, 20.) It also gave them a new scale of values. When the Apostles had been scourged before the Sanhedrin they went out 'rejoicing that they had been found worthy to suffer indignity for the sake of the Name.' (Acts 5 : 41.)

During the time that had passed since his Resurrection day, they had been learning to rely more and more on the reality of his *unseen* Presence and leadership. And now, although they would see his Face and hear his Voice no more in this world, they had reached the stage when they could understand that he would still be with them and would, in fact, be able to help them more powerfully than before.

The fifth century theologian, St. Leo, makes the very pregnant comment [1] that at the Ascension 'that which was visible in our Redeemer *passed into sacraments*.' He also points out that the disciples had to learn to recognize their Master not

[1] In his second sermon on the Ascension, which is appointed to be read, both in the Sarum and in the modern Roman Breviary, at Matins on the Saturday after Ascension Day.

only as Man but also, in the completest sense, as God; and they could hardly have done this so long as he continued to appear to them in a human form. 'They were no longer hindered by an object of bodily sight from directing their minds to the truth that he had not absented himself from the Father by coming down to earth, nor departed from his disciples by ascending.'

These consequences of the Ascension are matters of great importance, for the Church and for the world. But the reader may perhaps feel that they are rather remote from his everyday life and interests. So we come to our third question.

3. *What difference does the Ascension make to us?*

The best answer is the one which is given at the beginning of the third chapter of the Epistle to the Colossians. 'Were you not raised to life with Christ? Then aspire to the realm above, where Christ is, seated at the right hand of God, and let your thoughts dwell on that higher realm, not on this earthly life. I repeat, you died; and now your life is hidden with Christ in God.'

This language may sound unreal to most people, and even to most Christians, to-day. Yet it is nothing more than a plain statement of New Testament Christianity. On certain occasions, it may be on Sundays, and especially after receiving Holy Communion, we twentieth-century Christians may draw a little nearer to that life which is hidden with Christ because it is a sharing in his heavenly life. But to say 'I am like a dead man so far as this world is concerned, because my thoughts, my hopes and my interests are centred in the higher world where Christ lives and reigns'—that would be, for most of us, quite unreal as a description of our everyday lives. Need we look any further to discover the reason why the Christian Faith is spreading less rapidly in the twentieth century than it did in the first?

For our encouragement, let us call to mind the historic fact that large numbers of people, who were very much like ourselves to begin with, have succeeded in living that life, and have found it perfectly real. In not a few instances it has at last shone through their features so clearly that even their portraits or photographs, after they are dead, still bear witness to the ascended Christ. They succeeded in living the Christian life because that was what they wanted to do more than anything else in the world. It was this, more than anything else, that they 'let their thoughts dwell on.'

When the New Testament writers say that the life of Christ is in the Christian, they are not speaking metaphorically. The life of Christ is in us because of our baptism. It has been strengthened in us by every good communion we have made, and by repeated acts of faith and prayer. We are asking for something that is quite real when we pray that 'our sinful bodies may be made clean by his Body, and our souls washed through his most precious Blood, and that we may evermore dwell in him and he in us.'

Many people possess some particular gift of mind or character which they have inherited from their parents. That is not an exact parallel, for the life of our parents is not in us as the life of Christ is in us. But even in that case, we realize that the part that any inherited talent plays in our lives will depend on the use we ourselves make of it—on how far we give it a chance.

This life that is in the Christian believer is a risen and ascended life. When the apostle says, 'Let your thoughts dwell on that higher realm, not on this earthly life,' he is only repeating in other words what our Lord himself had said— 'Set your mind on God's kingdom and his justice before everything.' (Matthew 6 : 33.)

If it is not one thing that captures a man's mind it will be another. 'Where your wealth is, there will your heart be also.' (Matthew 6 : 21.) The ruling passion, the idea which dominates the imagination and continually returns to mind, will shape a man's life after its own pattern more and more as the years go by. For some, it is money ; for others, fame ;

for others, worldly importance either for themselves or for their children. For many, at the present time, it is pleasure, because although they know that the things on which they 'set their minds' will soon pass away, they have no belief in anything that will not pass away.

We do not need to be more than moderately observant to notice that the pursuit of these objectives does not in fact bring lasting satisfaction, peace of mind, or a sense of fulfilment. There is a need in man's nature which cannot be met by any of these, or by all of them together. It was to meet that need that the Saviour of men was crucified. It was to meet that need, also, that 'the third day he rose again from the dead; he ascended into heaven, and sitteth at the right hand of God the Father Almighty.'

What, then, ought to be the ruling passion, the idea which dominates the imagination of every Christian believer? I shall give the answer in another man's words, partly because I cannot help feeling my own unworthiness, partly because the man in question lived at a time which was almost as worldly as our own, but chiefly because the words are so plain and practical, and yet say all that the most sincere Christian can need.

'You must make it the great point of your ambition (and a nobler view you cannot entertain) to be a living image of Christ; that, so far as circumstances will allow, even those who have heard and read but little of him may, by observing you, in some measure see and know what kind of life the life of Jesus was. And this must be your constant care, your prevailing character, as long as you live.' [1]

[1] Philip Doddridge, *The Rise and Progress of Religion,* ch. 6.

12

ADD TO THE PROOFS

EVEN after more than nineteen centuries of Christian witness we still sometimes hear people repeat the well-worn statement, 'No one has ever come back to tell us.' Every time we say the Creed we are reminded that this statement is untrue. There is one Person who passed through the gate of death and did come back for that very purpose—to tell us all we need to know.

The Resurrection of Jesus was a unique happening. It was not a mere reanimation of the Body. He did not return to the old conditions of life. He rose from the dead in such a way that he could die no more. Death had lost its dominion over him. (Rom. 6 : 9.) It was in a changed Body, which could no longer grow old or die or decay, that he came back to his handful of faithful followers. And he did not come back to them once only. He did not give them merely a passing glimpse of his risen Body, which could be mistaken for a vision or a hallucination. He came to them at various times throughout a period of forty days and told them how his work in the world was to be carried on into the future. (Acts 1 : 3.)

It was these appearances of their risen Master to the first Christian witnesses, and the power that came to them through the promised gift of the Holy Spirit, that set the Church in motion. It can safely be claimed that nothing else except a real contact with a risen divine and human Lord can adequately account for the lives of the saints, or indeed for the lives of countless numbers of other good Christians, belonging to every generation since the date of the Resurrection of Jesus.

That Resurrection was different from everything else that

has happened in the history of the world; and the results that have followed from it are different from everything else that has happened in the history of the world.

Those results first showed themselves in the men to whom the risen Christ had appeared. On the feast of Pentecost they went out into the streets of Jerusalem, crowded with Jewish pilgrims from many lands, and began to give their public witness. Peter was their leader and the chief spokesman. 'The Jesus we speak of has been raised by God,' he said, 'as we can all bear witness.' (Acts 2 : 32.) And on that first day about three thousand people believed that witness and were baptized—a wonderful beginning of a mighty harvest which is still being reaped.

Why did so many accept the message? They knew that Jesus had been put to death, and since the day of his death these people who were listening had seen and heard nothing more of him. Now a little group of men were telling them that he had risen from the dead. It was no more an easy message for them to accept than it would be for us if we were hearing it for the first time. The witnesses were obviously not learned men, not practised speakers, not important people according to any worldly ways of reckoning importance. Why did three thousand people believe an apparently incredible statement on the very first day that it was made by such men as these?

It seems clear that we must find the answer to that question in the words with which St. Peter followed up his announcement of the Lord's Resurrection. 'Exalted thus with God's right hand, he received the Holy Spirit from the Father, as was promised, and all that you now see and hear flows from him.' (Acts 2 : 33.)

It was some visible change in these men, some obvious marks of the effect that had been worked in them by their Master's Resurrection, which made their message credible. It was to these signs that the witnesses could point in support of their testimony.

In the first place there was the surprising fact that such men as these were giving public testimony, and were finding effective words for it. They claimed to have received the Holy Spirit, and there was visible and audible evidence that this claim was true. They were speaking words which, in such men as they were, seemed to imply the influence of a higher power. It was clear not only that they themselves were completely certain about the happening to which they bore witness but also that they were under some form of inward compulsion to bear witness to it. In spite of their determination to be attended to, and to get their message across, they showed no wish to exalt themselves, no sensitiveness about their personal feelings. Their concern was for the welfare of those who heard them. Their motive was that motive which Christians were soon to recognize and rank first of all and to call 'charity'—a disinterested love of God and of all men for God's sake. In short, it was the fire of the Holy Spirit in these first Christian witnesses which caused men to believe their words.

I once knew a man whose wife had been cured, very rapidly and by prayer alone, from a disease which medical specialists had pronounced to be incurable. The result was that he wanted to tell every one about the wonderful thing that had happened. He bore his witness quietly and without any trace of self-assertion. Even if I had not known that the fact was true, I think the effect that it had on this man would in itself have convinced me that something remarkable had happened. I can only describe it by saying that there was a light on his face which compelled one to take him seriously. It seems natural to picture an effect of that same kind, and much greater in degree, in these first Christian witnesses, not only on the day of Pentecost but through the days and years that followed. There is no need to underestimate the part which was played by their works of healing, in persuading people to accept their message. But that was only one sign of a greater factor which was always present—the power of the Holy Spirit, working with them and through them.

Without this, the Christian Church would have died in its
cradle. The bare statement that Jesus had risen, however con-
fidently it might be made, would not have been believed
unless some evidence that it was true had been visible in those
who bore witness to it. But they could go on to say 'All that
you now see and hear flows from him'—this divine influence
which has made life new for us, this power from God which
you now feel to be at work and which you can share with us
if you will believe with us.

It has always been so. Whenever Christians have submitted
their whole lives to the claims of the risen Christ, whenever
they have allowed the Holy Spirit to set their hearts on fire
for him, there the witness has been received and the Faith has
spread. It will be so again. It can be so to-day. If the Church
has grown weak in this century it is not because people have
become harder hearted or more sceptical by nature than they
used to be. We who profess the Christian Faith must look for
the reason at least partly in ourselves.

'The Jesus we speak of has been raised by God as we can
all bear witness.' It is a tremendous statement to make. The
world will not accept our witness until we can point to great
results, or until great results become noticeable, whether we
point to them or not. When people begin to notice a change
in us who believe, a course of life which rises above the
motives of this world, an earnestness which compels respect
for the honour of God and, with all this, a new kindness in
our judgments and a new eagerness to help all who are in
trouble, including those who have offended or harmed us—
then we shall not need to say 'all that you now see and hear
flows from him.' For it is the risen Christ alone who can work
this change in the nature of men.

We can find the same good reasons for accepting the witness of the Church to our Lord's Resurrection as the first
converts found. We can find reasons for accepting it in the
written evidence of the New Testament and in the history of
the last nineteen hundred years. But both of these lines of

evidence need to be supplemented by a third—the results which have been brought about in the lives of Christian believers. If we will look for those results we can still find them, in the world of our own day, and in some of the people we know.

But no Christian should be content to stop at that point. We are intended to recognize the working of this power in our own lives and to know it by our own experience. We shall do so if we dedicate our lives to our divine Master, seeking and longing after, and faithfully following, the guidance of the Holy Spirit.

Good Churchpeople show their loyalty to Christ in many ways. They bear the witness of public worship on Sundays, and that is not always an easy thing to do. They try to regulate their lives by Christian standards of conduct, not by the standards of the present age. By their offerings, and even more by their prayers and active co-operation, it is the laity who are keeping God's Church alive.

There is one thing more which could be done, and it would make all the difference. That one thing more is to let our divine Master have his will with us and make us *fervent* Christians, on fire with our religion, so that it becomes the motive-force of our lives and the constant background to our thoughts. That is the purpose of the Holy Spirit for us. 'Come, Holy Ghost, fill the hearts of thy faithful people, and kindle in them the fire of thy love.'

We are called to make our own contribution to the proofs. When St. John Vianney was told that a certain lady, whose piety was rather superficial, would like some holy relics, he answered with mordant homour 'Let her make some.' A similar challenge comes to us to add to the evidence of our Lord's Resurrection which we can see has existed, and still exists, in the lives of men and woman.

There is one practice which, I believe, is more likely than any other to make this possible. It is to take our New Testament into some quiet place, at home or in church, and then to think over and pray over the words we read. If we are in earnest about this and try to make our thoughts as realistic as we can, we shall in effect be opening the door to the Holy Spirit. Time spent alone with God, in prayer and meditation and earnest seeking—it is this that can set hearts on fire.

INDEX

STUDIES IN CHRISTIAN FAITH AND PRACTICE

THE Resurrection of Jesus must be accepted as an historical event, attested not only by the New Testament but also by a great weight of collateral evidence—the birth, growth and continuing life of the Church, the witness of saints and martyrs, the day-to-day experience of countless believing Christians. The Biblical accounts, from the discovery of the Empty Tomb to the Ascension, are seen in the context of the results which have followed from the event; and the event itself is seen as God's answer to all human problems. The Old Testament revelation, the doctrine of the future life, Baptism, the Eucharist, the mission of the Church and the present needs of the world are considered in the light of the Resurrection. The writer's chief concern is to show how these various aspects of the subject are related to our lives to-day, and how each reader can verify the evidence for himself.

The author is Vicar of Boston, Lincs, and Canon of Lincoln. He has written a number of well-known theological works as well as some verse. He was awarded the Cambridge University Seatonian prize eleven times.